D1176545

Tonalá

Tonalá

Conservatism, Responsibility, and Authority in a Mexican Town

MAY N. DIAZ

University of California Press
Berkeley Los Angeles London
1970

University of California Press
Berkeley and Los Angeles, California
University of California Press
London, England

International Standard Book Number 0-520-00321-7 (clothbound edition)
0-520-01750-1 (paperbound edition)
Library of Congress Catalog Card Number: 66-14566
Designed by Theo Jung
Drawings by Steven Johnson
Second printing
First paperbound edition
Printed in the United States of America

PREFACE

The research for this book was undertaken as part of a larger study of culture change which was directed by Professor George M. Foster of the Department of Anthropology, University of California, Berkeley. My own phase of the project was concerned with an examination of the effect of industrialization of an urban center upon a nearby small community—of the expanding city of Guadalajara, Mexico, upon a conservative village or town within easy commuting distance. The field research from August, 1959 to August, 1960 was supported financially through a grant of the National Science Foundation. For an additional summer's fieldwork in 1962 I received financial assistance from the University of California Committee on Faculty Research. Funds for the preparation of the manuscript were made available by the Institute of Social Science of the University of California.

My debts of gratitude are many: to Professor Foster for his help and suggestions as well as for his willingness to allow his students to be independent in developing their own ideas and making their own mistakes; to Professor Robert F. Murphy who was an unfailing source of encouragement and intellectual stimulation and whose wit brightened the years of graduate training; to my patient students who listened while I developed and crystallized the analysis in lectures. I wish also to thank Richard Currier for his help in editing the final version of the manuscript. My debt of gratitude to the members of my family—who were participants, critics, and co-workers—is greater than I can express.

CONTENTS

I. WE GO TO FIND A VILLAGE

ONE OF THE MOST significant developments of the second half of the twentieth century has been the emergence and growth of industrial economies in parts of Asia, Africa, and Latin America, regions traditionally viewed as sources of raw materials for the West rather than as producers of manufactured items. Equally significant have been efforts of nations to move themselves into the industrial world through economic and social planning. These efforts have been marked by varying degrees of success and of unrest and conflict; they have affected sectors of society in multifarious ways and to differing degrees. The changes wrought by rapid industrialization have provided a challenging area of study for social scientists from many disciplines.

The major aspects of the process of industrialization have been studied primarily by economists and sociologists, while political scientists have concerned themselves with the dynamics of new national politics. Anthropologists, on the other hand, have joined with other social scientists in examining the nature of culture change in general and of industrialization in particular, but from somewhat different perspectives. One group of studies has been concerned with ascertaining the social and cultural changes which come to traditional societies around the world as a response to economic growth. Other studies have examined in detail the responses of individual communities.

The large literature on community development bears witness to an increasing awareness of the cultural factors that aid or impede programs of technical assistance. Anthropologists have pointed out in study after study the discrepancy between the traditional ways of life of rural people all over the world and the goals and methods employed by planners trained in industrial societies and socialized in an urban culture.

Industrialization begins in the city, is developed by city people, is part of the city culture, and as it proceeds, goes hand in hand with urbanization. For these reasons anthropologists working in peasant villages have seldom found it necessary to ask why villages do not industrialize, why villages seldom develop themselves, and why many of them are only marginally involved in the national industrial system as either producers or consumers. The first question has come to the mind of countless travelers from the nineteenth century on, who, in the face of stagnation in the provinces, have answered that the sloth, ignorance, and shiftlessness of the peasants are to blame for the lag in development. The second question is implicit in the very idea of working out a community development program, while the last is of increasing concern to national-policy makers. Political officials, technical-aid specialists, and economists are faced with the need to accelerate the process of transforming the byways of their own country to main roads of national development. Max Weber (1947: p. 167) outlined the central feature of the problem:

A high degree of traditionalism in habits of life, such as characterized by the labouring classes in early modern times, has not sufficed to prevent a great increase in the rationalization of economic enterprises under capitalistic direction. The same was, for instance, true of the socialistic rationalization of the taxation system of Egypt. Nevertheless, this traditionalistic attitude had to be overcome in the Western World before the further development to the specifically modern type of rational capitalistic economy could take place.

Although a nation's industrialization and economic development can proceed despite the traditionalism of some of its people, when the gap between urban and rural sectors widens beyond a crucial (if undetermined) point, nations find themselves in a crisis. What can be glossed over verbally as a "lag" becomes the basis of political controversy as, for example, in Italy. It becomes the source of difficulty in socialist nations with planned economies, and one of the underlying causes of populist revolts elsewhere.

In a study of a south Italian village Edward C. Banfield raised the question: "What are the elements in the village which impede its development?" His conclusions were that the difficulty lay in the villagers' inability to organize themselves and to "act for the common good" (Banfield, 1958: pp. 7–12). The lack of political organization stemmed in turn from the ethos of "amoral familism," that is, the absence of responsibility and commitment to indivduals and groups outside the nuclear family. The ethos was a response to a high death rate, certain land tenure conditions, and the absence of the institution of the extended family.

Although the analysis fits the behavioral data as well as those obtained by projective tests, it falls somewhat short as an answer to the question originally posed. Two questions, neither of which completely invalidate the study, suggest that further analysis is necessary. First, the argument is circular. Amoral familism leads to a lack of solidarity which in turn leads to the maximization of the nuclear family, and around we go again. The problem here is a logical one and is a problem only if we are concerned with analysis or generalization. Circular statements about empirical events need not be invalid even though they violate the canons of Western logic, for, indeed, human institutions are often tautological, human activities often insist upon themselves, and culture is often redundant, though not superfluous. One is reminded of an episode in an old Sacha Guitry movie in which three robbers, having stolen seven pearls, sat down to divide the spoils. One begins the distribution, "One for you and one for you and one for me; one for you and one for you and *two* for me."

The two who were shorted protest, "Why do you get three pearls when each of us gets only two?"

"Because I am the leader."

"And why are you the leader?"

"Because I have three pearls."

At an analytic level we encounter the second difficulty: namely, that amoral familism is not of itself an identifiable phenomenon, but a category useful as an intermediate step in the construction of paradigms or hypotheses. It should not be invoked as an explanation. It has been suggested that it might be useful to reverse the paradigm: a series of historical events led to the development of a particular kind of economic and political power structure; consequently, generations of villagers learned from similar kinds of experiences that they must "maximize the nuclear family," for to do otherwise was to sacrifice it.

This study is directed toward Banfield's kind of question. What are the elements in a Mexican peasant village which impede economic development? Or to phrase it differently, how does the village function to preserve its traditional ways despite the exploding industrialization of the surrounding region? The corollary question must also be touched on: by what means and in what ways is the village affected by the urban and national economic system?

The particular case under examination is that of Tonalá, a town of peasants and potters located ten miles from the city of Guadalajara in west central Mexico. Perhaps the case of Tonalá is not a unique one. Some of its structural features may well be typical of other rural and provincial entities in Latin America, so that by looking at one town closely we may begin to find the regularities which not only characterize and define villages, but which maintain them as villages while cities expand, explode, and dominate the life of nations.

My first view of the village which was to be my home for a year came at the end of the summer of 1959 when my husband and I were touring small towns and villages within a twenty-mile radius of Guadalajara in the state of Jalisco to find a suitable location for the study. The tour was time-consuming and both exhaustive and exhausting, for the choice of place in which to work is a delicate and crucial matter. The final success of the fieldwork may hinge upon the happy selection of a community both willing to tolerate strangers and appropriate to the requirements of the study. Several villages which had looked feasible when we pored over maps and censuses in Berkeley had to be ruled out: they had been swallowed up by the city or were surrounded by subdivisions and could no longer be considered self-contained communities, they were too small or too large, and a few had been left neglected or abandoned as history passed them by, so that a year's stay would have been a period of penance among the eroding remains of a forgotten community.

The greatest problem, however, was what seemed like a simple matter: finding a village with an available vacant house. Our plans were for our entire family to move into the community—my husband, my two boys, and myself—and try to become insofar as possible another family unit living in a community of families.

Professor George M. Foster of the University of California at Berkeley, under whose supervision I was working, had suggested that we try to settle in a pottery-making town, for often it is easier to gain entry into a town of craftsmen, who are interested in talking of their skills and selling their wares, rather than into a community of farmers, wary of tax assessors and suspicious of possible government agents. Pottery work also provides a built-in framework for interviewing. On the basis of three criteria—the village must still exist as an independent entity, there must be a house available, and there must be some means of getting to know people—we choose the town of Tonalá.

We moved into the village in October, 1959, and remained there until the beginning of August, 1960. My field staff was my family. Although mine was the final reponsibility for gathering all materials, since I was the only anthropologist, on many occasions we were able to work together as a team, thus obtaining data usually considered men's material, as well as women's, adults', and children's. Information on the life of village children when unobserved by adults, interesting and plentiful at first, was gradually reduced to a trickle as my sons became Tonaltecan, rather than Berkeley, children. Fortunately, our house remained a favorite playground of the neighborhood, so there was still an avenue whereby hypotheses on the behavior of children could be checked against observations in several contexts.

Our methods of study were primarily the time-honored anthropological field techniques. We were as much participants as observers. Villagers who were curious about our presence were told that I was studying their pottery-making, for indeed I was very much interested in it. A few people assumed that I was doing some kind of historical research, for many villagers are proud of the fact that Tonalá already existed when the Spaniards came. I tried to do my work without upsetting the status quo and without being associated with any particular set or faction. Often the attempt to remain neutral in the shifting alliances and conflicts in the town was like walking a tight-rope stretched over a cataract, but on the whole we managed to remain on friendly terms with school, church, and town hall. I doubted, however, whether it would be possible to maintain one's neutrality for very long, and by the end of our stay I was beginning to feel that eventually a showdown would come when we would have to take sides.

We participated in several spheres of Tonalá life. My children were enrolled in the town school and went through the usual course of instruction for their ages. Although they knew only a few sentences of Spanish before their arrival, within a month or so they were able to get along quite well in class and on the playground. Stephen (age seven) joined the drum and bugle corps and was allowed to lead the school parades. Robert (age ten), along with the older boys in school, helped with the many chores which fall on the shoulders of Tonaltecan students: going to the city to buy foodstuffs sold to the pupils during morning recess, sweeping the earth play yard, and watering down the dust in the corridors and patios.

Before the end of the year they had the good fortune of participating in many of the activities we look on with nostalgia as belonging to the lost age of the last century. They had helped water the elephants of the traveling circus, they had gleaned peanuts in the fields and eaten them warm after roasting on a bonfire, and they had been cowhands and goatherds. But most fully of all, they had taken part in the constant small commerce and trade of the village. They had sold lemonade on our doorstep to passersby, and they had peddled oranges at the soccer game at the edge of town. Like other village boys, they had rented out their comic books on Sundays in the plaza and had carried bundles for elderly ladies getting off the bus. Their activities revealed nuances and flavors of town life that adult observers might miss.

As members of a functioning household we found ourselves plunged into another set of activities. Like any Tonalá family, we had to cope with the problems of buying food and supplies, of obtaining water, and thereby we became aware that such seemingly simple problems are both time-consuming and difficult to solve. Much of my daily round was that of the Tonaltecan housewife, as I traveled from church to kitchen to *tortillería* (tortilla shop). Like the average man of the town, my husband spent less time in church and more time in the plaza listening to talk about village affairs.

It was from the latter kind of informal fieldwork that we became involved more directly with municipal affairs. Many townsmen were convinced that local political officeholders could never function effectively as leaders because of their multiple commitments to relatives and friends. They were ready, many even enthusiastically concerned, to ferret out some outsider who would be willing to take the initiative as a leader in municipal affairs, and approached my husband, a Jalisciense himself, to persuade him to take an active role in local politics. He decided to cooperate to the extent of attending committee meetings, participating in discussions, going along on deputations to the governor of the state, and generally acting as chauffeur when necessary, but he felt that it would be unfair to the townspeople for him to assume a role he could not continue later through a period when projects that had been initiated would have to be maintained. It would be wiser to try to bolster local leadership. From my point of view it also seemed more advisable, for I would be watching Tonaltecan politics in action.

A great deal of my working time was spent in informal social affairs. I regularly visited about fifteen households. Although these families did not comprise a random sample, they did represent different social ranks, typical Tonalá occupations, varying age groups, the literate and the illiterate, native villagers and "strangers," and residents from all four *barrios* (neighborhoods) of the town. Several times a week I attended a sewing and gossip session. In addition, during the course of the year we were invited to almost the full roster of life-cycle ceremonies and other festivities as well.

Much of the information reported on was obtained during the course of visits, fiestas, and informal conversations. Since I wanted to keep things as relaxed as possible, I gradually learned the technique of memorizing the content of conversations and then writing up notes immediately afterward. With some practice one can reproduce fairly good transcripts—at least of occasions lasting no longer than an hour, a fact which in part accounts for the growing restlessness of the anthropologist when a gathering drags on and on. Imminent mnemonic confusion threatens him.

For many kinds of information, however, it is necessary to use regular informants (or advisers, as my husband suggests). Although many townspeople had the patience and courtesy to put up with my questions, I am particularly indebted to Magdalena Covarrubias, Isidoro Ramos, and the Melchor family—Salvador and Alejandra especially. Like most anthropologists, I feel that the informants I worked with were most remarkable people. They combined intelligence and perceptiveness with the warmth of true friendship, and I am grateful to have known them.

Our interviewing techniques were varied. Sometimes I asked open-ended questions which I hoped would call forth answers revealing attitudes, interests, and emotions rather than simple informational responses. Some interviews were more tightly structured. These were of two kinds. The most successful procedure was one whereby my husband and I played complementary roles, he guiding the conversation into the channels of interest to me and I mentally noting responses and reactions of others to them. This system worked particularly well because he was able to employ the parables, riddles, jokes, and anecdotes dear to the heart of the rural Mexican to elicit frank and free discussions. In a second kind of structured interview, I worked alone, having prepared a schedule to remind me of the questions I wanted answers to; but I tried to keep the setting informal enough to allow the digressions and parenthetical remarks which are often the most revealing part of an interview.

Questionnaires were used only in taking a census. During the second half of our stay I decided it was necessary to know the exact composition of households and to obtain fairly accurate occupational data, for the published federal census did not cover such matters as residential patterns. We then embarked on a census, a rather ambitious ethnographic undertaking, for Tonalá has a population of more than 5,000. The census had three phases: preparation, blanketing, and mop-up. First I had to find a compromise between what I wanted to know and what the villagers were willing to respond to. In order not to prejudice the entire project, I omitted questions on such matters as land tenure and income. During the preparation phase, the census sheets were printed in Guadalajara, and I enlisted the aid of the elementary school director, Sr. Isidoro Ramos, and the curate of the parish church, the Reverend Carlos Gonzalez Becerra. The census was of interest to them both, to increase their knowledge of their students and parishioners respectively, and they were also interested in furthering social science research.

As census takers we used the members of the school's sixth-grade class. This procedure, although by no means ideal for a model census, was a workable solution for a practical enumeration. Most of the children were between fourteen and sixteen years of age, and they were all used to recording information with pencil and paper—a fact untrue of their elders. They were given a briefing by the school director and sent out to gather information for the block in which they lived as a pre-test. These census sheets were then checked by the sixth-grade teacher to be sure instructions were being followed, and by one of my regular informants and myself to be sure the information obtained was accurate.

Phase Two then began. All census takers were assigned a number of blocks. Gathering this information was considered part of the students' social studies assignment, so there was motivation to work other than their eagerness to participate in something they had been told was important.

Phase Three began when the great mass of sheets was turned over to me. First I toured the town and recorded the number of every occupied house. This task was less simple than it seems, for often it was difficult to decide whether a jumble of adobes represented an occupied dwelling or not. The numbers were then checked against the census sheets, and lists of houses for which we lacked information were given to small corps of eager sixth-grade boys, who were paid to bring in the missing data. Almost all sheets were also checked with Magdalena Covarrubias and Alejandra Melchor, who had an encyclopedic knowledge of their fellow villagers. They added to the roster the names of toddlers and infants, who were often omitted, and they were almost always able to clear up any mysteries as to kinship relations. However, I soon had to give up all hope of finding out the exact ages of the townspeople; neither informants, family members, nor the persons concerned knew chronological ages. In the end, out of a total of nine hundred households, there were forty or so for which we had no information. The priest offered to obtain that material, and census sheets for almost all those households were mailed to me after my return to Berkeley. In return for the generous cooperation of both the Reverend Sr. Gonzalez and Sr. Ramos I supplied them with copies of the completed census sheets.

The only additional technique I employed was that of having school children write themes on open-ended topics. Unfortunately, I decided on this procedure too late in the school year to obtain more than one set of papers, and they were too abbreviated to be of much use for analysis. In the summer of 1963 John Ingham undertook as a short-term field project the administration of projective tests in Tonalá, and in the fall he completed the analysis of the responses. This research is reported on elsewhere (Ingham, 1964).

The heavy reliance upon the anthropological technique of participant observation rather than standardized sociological procedures stems from an ingrained preference for watching people in action. I am also convinced that behavioral data is more meaningful when it is observed in its cultural context. Aside from my anthropological bias, I brought to the fieldwork the background of a seventeen-year intensive acquaintanceship with Mexican culture and a long-term knowledge of the state of Jalisco in particular.

Hopefully, this experience serves as a check and control of data obtained on social occasions. The observer of human behavior is always watching a process in which individuals accommodate their role-playing and readjust their expectations to the actions of others, whether fellow villagers, census takers, or anthropologist observers. One can often only surmise the true state of reality as informants circumvent tender spots or erect barricades around them (cf. Berreman, 1962). Or one can equally be led astray by villagers who use anthropologists for their own social or psychological ends, so that one becomes primarily and naïvely the bolsterer of the insecure or the tool of the skillful manipulator. But a long stay, an awareness that there are subtleties, that actions have several levels of meaning, and a background of anthropological training should help to offset the traps that lie in wait for the observer.

II. OF TIME AND THE SEASONS

FROM JUNE THROUGH OCTOBER is the rainy season, the time when the earthen floors and the adobe walls of the houses of Tonalá turn a rich gray-brown from the moisture which they absorb, and between the cobblestones of the streets grass springs up almost overnight. The skies are various: electric blue with white pillows of clouds like those in a child's coloring book, black and indigo as if carrying omens of evil, flaming, opaline, pallid. In a few days after the first rain, basins and hollows are filled with water, while along the lanes leading out of town bougainvillea and morning-glories brighten earth walls and clamber over *guamúchil* trees (*Pithecolobium dulce* or *Inga pungens*).

It rains daily. In the afternoons the streets become rivers, and children rush out to wade in the streams. At the beginning of the season even adults wet their feet in the rushing water, young ladies tucking up their skirts and laughing coquettishly. In the principal streets large cobblestones are laid to allow pedestrians to cross, much in the manner that ancient Romans used stepping stones to pass over open storm sewers. There is something Roman too about the carved stone lintels over doors and windows in a few Tonalá houses, and as in an ancient ruined city they suggest more prosperous days of the past. In some cases they bridge the opening of a house whose walls are disintegrating, or they stand over a collapsed pile of adobe, surrounded by growing weeds.

In the blocks around the central plaza the dwellings are larger than those at the edge of town. Each succeeding rain stains and erodes the plastered walls, and colors become muted. The single stories stand fifteen or twenty feet high to provide security or isolation for their inhabitants. Whether Spanish or *criollo* (creole) bourgeosie built high walls in past centuries to guard themselves against the Indian population of the town, or whether the walls were added in the years of insecurity during the Revolution is not clear, but this style continues as one of the building traditions. It is the Mediterranean house, which encloses a family, shuts it off from its neighbors, and opens only to the sky, so that the properly cloistered woman of the house sees only a patch of blue; neither horizon nor neighbor is visible to her. We lived in a house of this kind, and on days when I was troubled with nostalgia or loneliness, I felt that the arched portals of my patio were a New World replica of medieval nunneries and monasteries. This was not the architecture calling up song and abandon as in the stereotype of Latin-American life presented in the motion pictures of the 'thirties and 'forties; it was rather a style suggesting meditation, asceticism, and the cold comfort of stone.

The second kind of house is more typically Tonaltecan —a low, adobe, single-roomed structure, presenting a wall, a door, and a window to the street, open to the center of the block behind its façade. These houses share a common compound and look onto fields of maize.

The third kind of house has only lately begun to appear in town. It is a modest version of the contemporary urban home—the latest descendant of the Central European International Style. The architect-designed houses of Guadalajara draw their aestheic value from an interplay of form and shadow through the dramatic juxtaposition of solid shapes and the contrast of textures. At their best they are bold and arresting. The economy version in small towns, however, repeats the clichés of the style without attention to proportions: bright, plastered walls, cubelike structures, and the ubiquitous planter. There are only two or three of these as yet in Tonalá; their importance lies not in their numbers, but in the fact that they represent the townspeople's view of the modern middle-class dwelling.

The public buildings cluster around the central plaza, an indifferently attended garden with a kiosk in the middle. Most conspicuous of all is the new market, erected in 1962, which provides shelter for the vendors of pottery, fruits, and vegetables. It is two-storied, built of brick and concrete, and covered with a zigzag roof, a common architectural feature of new Mexican markets. To one side stands the town hall, containing the offices of the mayor, the secretary, and the police, as well as a meeting room officially known as "the library" but without books. A large, enclosed yard adjoins where cows and donkeys found wandering on the city streets are incarcerated until the owners pay their fines.

Along the same street rises the Church of the Sacred

Heart, an empty shell no longer used for services, looming stucco-white and yellow against the western sky, its pointed arches, three flat bell-towers, and palm tree vaguely unreal as if they were all part of a Hollywood set. Tonalá's church, just off the main plaza, is, on the other hand, less theatrical. It is large, built of dark stone in the sturdy, restrained style of the eighteenth century. A flying buttress on the north side is dated 1731, but parts of the structure were probably built earlier. The building on the south side, now housing the public elementary school, was originally a monastery and still suggests its original purpose in its parade of stately arches.

Across the street stands a new building very much of the twentieth century—the health center. Here, in a cement and glass building, a public health nurse employed by the federal government sees patients, instructs in child care, and dispenses some medication.

Whereas the presence of these public facilities indicates that we are dealing with a town rather than a village, the rural world is not far away. A few blocks in any direction, beyond the edge of town, lie the fields of growing corn. In August, when we first arrived, the tassels were already formed, and the *milpa* (corn in the fields) was almost tall enough to shield a man, a fact of interest to lovers and thieves. All around lie the rolling hills, eroded and inarable, patched with green grass and pocked with the water holes that supply drinking water.

In the rainy season the countryside of Tonalá looks soft and bucolic. It would have inspired pastoral odes if the town had produced a poet; instead the artistic talents of its inhabitants have been expressed in crafts and in music. For at least three centuries it has produced some of the finest pottery made in Mexico, and some Tonaltecans have made pieces that in shape and decoration are objects of art.

They also have a long tradition as musicians. The Augustinian Father Basalenque commented in the seventeenth century (Basalenque, 1886) on the high quality of the music in the parochial church, while from at least the last century on, Tonalá has been a provider of bands and orchestras for the festivals of surrounding towns. In the past, the climax of one of the town fiestas was a musical contest between bands representing different barrios, which lasted until one group was left the victor as the others gave up through physical exhaustion. Festivals all over the state are still enlivened with Tonalá music. In addition, several Tonaltecans have studied seriously; a concert pianist, three members of the Guadalajara symphony orchestra, and two of the Jalisco State Band count Tonalá as their place of birth.

The dry season provides inspiration for neither poets nor musicians; for pottery makers it is a time of work. The end of the rainy season marks harvest time, a period of great agricultural activity and, in a good year, of prosperity for those Tonaltecans who work land. From December on, pottery-making keeps most of the townspeople busy. Gradually the dry air desiccates the green grass and plants, until by March only the nopal cactus and the guamúchil tree provide color in the countryside. March and April bring strong winds, and the loose dust of field and street swirls through town. When the air is cold, the children's feet and hands become chapped, sometimes crack and bleed. By May, however, the sun is hot, and clouds of flies rise from the streets as one passes by. The water from the wells grows brackish until it burns plants, and animals refuse to drink it. Each year some of the water holes are dry by the beginning of May; the townspeople struggle to obtain enough water, and housewives compete to buy whatever the *aguadores* (water vendors) bring in, crowding around the carts, pushing and shouting. The dust lies thick on unpaved roads, the flies buzz thickly in the heat.

The land was dry and warm too when the Spaniards came in March of 1530, but then the hills were dotted with oak trees, affording islands of shade. The conquistadores had traveled through the more heavily wooded lake region of Michoacán before reaching Tonalá, and in their eyes the plains of the latter region were a good and prosperous land (cf. Nuño de Guzmán and De Arceo quoted in Razo Zaragoza y Cortés, 1963: pp. 41, 249). The expedition that came to Tonalá was headed by Nuño de Guzmán, a man whose name became synonymous with the cruel conquistador, known even among his contemporaries for his arrogance and fierce temper. It was his intention to conquer the bellicose Chichimecas to the northwest and to find the legendary Amazons (Razo Zaragoza y Cortés, 1963: p. 17). The expedition consisted of a hundred and fifty cavalrymen, an approximately similar number of Spanish infantry, and seven or eight thousand Indians; it was a well-supplied army: ammunition, arms, small artillery, sandals for the infantry and Indians, extra clothing, two forges, iron, tools to build a ship if it became necessary, wine, vinegar, oil, flour, medicines, three thousand head of pigs, calves, and sheep, preserved meat, cheese. Having been blessed by Father Bartolomé de Estrada in Mexico City, they set off on what was to be a cruel, bloody journey of conquest and subjugation.

In Michoacán, Nuño demanded that the Tarascan king, Tangoaxan II, turn over his treasury and the women of his household, and then, dissatisfied with these spoils, he ordered the monarch tortured. When no more gold or silver was forthcoming, he set off in a fit of rage, taking the king along as hostage. On reaching the Lerma River, Nuño laid claim to the surrounding lands, and Tangoaxan was burned at the stake.

The news of Nuño de Guzmán's acts eventually reached the ancient kingdom of Tonalá. The queen, Tzihualpilli (or Tzapotzintli, if one refers to her by her personal name rather than title), regent for her minor son, ruled as symbolic head of a confederacy which included several villages around Lake Chapala, the settlements as far west as Tala, and was bounded to the southeast, east, and south by the deep gorge of the Santiago River. The area, although less extensive than that of the Tarascans of Michoacán, comprised the nucleus of what was to become the province of Nueva Galicia. The precise nature of the political unit of the Spaniards identified as the *Reinado de Tonalá* is not clear from the sources, but it seems not to have been a highly centralized monarchy. It was perhaps a loose confederation of settlements tied to the capital as subject villages in some cases and as satellites colonized by Tonaltecans in others (Anesagasti, 1899; Tello, 1891). On receiving word of the Spaniards' entry in Tonalá territory, the Queen and some of her councillors decided that the wiser course of action would be to welcome them and to offer their friendship. However, the *tastoanes* (in some sources *tacthuanes,* "captains" or "leaders") of several of the villages refused to accept what they saw as a cowardly decision and plotted in secret to oppose Nuño's army. One version of the subsequent events is recorded by Nuño himself in a letter sent to the Spanish monarch July 8, 1530. The account following is a paraphrased translation of this letter as it appears in Razo Zaragoza y Cortés' collection of documents relating to the conquest of Nueva Galicia.

Having sent some scouts ahead, Nuño started toward

the town of Tonalá. Along the way he was met by Tzihualpilli's messengers who informed him that a welcoming feast was prepared, and the loyal Tonaltecans were waiting to greet him, but that the rebellious villagers had stationed themselves near the town in a position to attack the Spaniards. Nuño's scouts corroborated this information. He went off to see for himself, and indeed the rebels were gathered together on a bare, rocky hill behind the town. To Nuño's greeting they responded truculently that they, in contrast to Tzihualpilli, would not offer birds in a feast, but arrows, if the Christians came toward them. Nuño divided his men into three groups, sending Cristóbal de Oñate with cavalry, infantry, and Indian allies around to the east side of the hill, Captain Verdugo with another group of Indians to the west, and he himself, guarded by artillery and infantry, approached the hill directly. His enemies fell back, retreating over the hill and into an area of orchards. It was a move of strategy rather than surrender, for they gave the Spaniards a hard battle, while assuring themselves of an escape route in the *barranca* (gorge). Nuño, certainly no Indian sympathizer ("they are not pretty, resembling devils"), praises their courage and fighting ability: ". . . and those who have been along in New Spain and other parts judge that they have not seen more daring and braver Indians than these." The casualties reported among the Spaniards were few; Nuño sent infantry and Indian allies in pursuit of the enemy hiding in the barranca, but they lost the trail in the rough terrain and returned. Nuño piously comments: "I returned well two hours after midday with all my people giving thanks to God for the mercy He had shown me; and I thought He approved what had been done" (Razo Zaragoza y Cortés, 1963: p. 41). Shortly thereafter Mass was celebrated by Fray Miguel de Padilla at the southwest edge of town where a temporary chapel was erected at a spot where presently there stands the Chapel of the White Cross. With Don Pedro Beltrán Nuño de Guzmán himself as godfather, Tzihualpilli was baptized and given the name Juana Bautista Danza (Anesagasti, 1899).

A simple story, but it has provided the raw stuff for the building of legends. Pious Tonaltecans today believe that the Indians were defeated because at the height of the battle St. James appeared riding his white horse across the sky, frightening the Indians and assuring the Spaniards they had supernatural support. In fact, Tonalá was renamed Santiago de Tonalá, and St. James became its patron saint. It is ironic that the patron of all Spain was placed in command over Indians, and doubly ironic that until ten years ago their defeat was annually re-enacted in the town fiesta when a Tonaltecan dressed as St. James wielded a whip, as my informants put it, "para dominar a los indios (in order to dominate the Indians)."

With time the Queen has grown younger and more beautiful. In 1530 one of the Spanish soldiers reported that as they approached the town, there came out of a house an ugly old Indian woman, claiming to be the Queen (Razo Zaragoza y Cortés, 1963: p. 290), hardly a flattering or effusive description of her appearance. By the end of the nineteenth century Tonaltecans were learning that it was her inherent wisdom and goodness which led her to accept Christianity, and that she served as a glorious model for all other heathens. By this century she is young and beautiful, and in the city pageants are built around her recalling the splendor of pre-Conquest Jalisco. Tzihualpilli appears in brilliant robes, her hair adorned with towering plumes; she is long of limb, fair of face, cultured, poetic, and noble. Another imposing female personage is added to that Mexican pantheon of symbolic maternal figures: the Virgin in all her manifestations, mothers real and imagined; and the legend grows.

But in Tonalá the legend also grows because there is little other historical material with which to fill the span of time, to give a sense of continuity, and to provide Tonaltecans with a sense of their existential importance.

Tonalá drops out of history; here and there a population figure indicates that it has shrunk considerably in size, or a mention is made in a document or a geography of Tonaltecan pottery. Since it has no rich natural resources to tempt Spanish entrepreneurs, no large non-Indian population to draw in men of substance and learning, it becomes an anonymous Indian village.

Only once again does it figure in written history. In 1541 the Chichimecas who lived across the barranca of the Santiago River rose in revolt against the Spaniards. Their timing was excellent. The province of Nueva Galicia found itself only weakly defended, for Coronado's expedition to the north had drawn off a large portion of available manpower (Simpson, 1960: p. 50), and the city of Guadalajara was in imminent danger of being attacked. The governor of the province, Juan de Oñate, having been defeated by the Chichimecas, retreated to the capital, where he fortified the city and took measures to assure himself of a corridor of retreat through the barranca to Tonalá, the only place he could count on to be friendly, according to the historian Navarrete (Navarrete, 1872).

In the meantime a Tonaltecan, Francisco Ganganilla, had been approached by the rebels and informed of their strategy in the hope of obtaining Tonaltecan cooperation. Men from Atemajac, Tequixtlan, Copalan, and Itzcatlan, villages like Tonalá lying between the barranca and the city, had promised to block the passage of the Spaniards on their way to Tonalá. The Tonaltecans, rather than joining the other Indians, captured thirty of their warriors and delivered them to Oñate. The Chichimecas were unable to effect the immediate victory they had hoped for, but they continued giving the Spaniards difficulty; eventually, however, the veteran troops of Viceroy Mendoza were able to crush the revolt. One is left with the uncomplimentary picture of sixteenth-century Tonaltecans as quislings. Perhaps during the colonial period Tonaltecans talked proudly of their aid to the Spaniards, but the incident does not figure in the present local historical tradition; no one remembers Francisco Ganganilla any more.

When Tonaltecans recall the past, they speak first of the Conquest, but secondly of the events in the first quarter of this century. Various happenings are inextricably mixed in the local view of things: the Revolution (1910–1920), World War I, the influenza epidemic, and the clerical counter-revolution (1926–1929). World War I did not, of course, directly affect Tonalá, but the townspeople believe that evil airs floated over the world from the corpses on the battlefield of Europe; these effluvia carried disease and misery around the globe and were responsible for the epidemic which killed hundreds of Tonaltecans. Old men report that so many people died that the living hardly had time to bury them, that grieving relatives would come in from outlying villages with dead bodies stacked on donkeys as if they were firewood. These events are engraved deeply in the memory of the older generation and are repeated when groups congregate to talk and tell stories, so the tales form part of the traditional learning of the young.

The Revolution figures in some stories, although few Tonaltecans took active part, for there were skirmishes nearby and people again remember seeing corpses. The *Cristero* movement, the pro-clerical revolt, forms a more important part of the history of Tonalá as viewed by the Tonaltecans, for many of them were violently partisan. Although the major military activity in Jalisco took place in Los Altos to the east and in the southern part of the state, the people of many rural areas were sympathetic to the religious party and provided support in the form of manpower, money, and information. The municipality of Tonalá was dominated by the pro-clerical faction, and inhabitants refused to cooperate with the government programs in education and community development. Many of them joined the Cristero forces and others (appropriately) did their part by praying. One such occasion occurred after the Cristeros had made a foray into the Guadalajara region and were returning to their Los Altos stronghold along the road which in those days ran along the edge of Tonalá. The government troops were in pursuit. As the story is told now, a group of townspeople locked themselves in the living quarters attached to the church and prayed for the safety of the Cristeros. Miraculously a fog appeared and slowed down the federals, and they were unable to catch the fleeing rebels. Some Tonaltecans claim to have seen St. James on horseback, shining white and splendid among the floating clouds in the sky. St. James has not appeared since. Even his image sallies forth no longer on the fiesta day in his honor. He hovers instead at the top of the main altarpiece in the parish church in a posture of eternal alarm. It was deemed sacrilegious to elevate a horse to the top of the retable, so now a dehorsed saint looks out over the faithful.

III. CITY AND TOWN

If one climbs from the northern edge of Tonalá to the top of the Cerro de Tzihualpilli, it is possible to look out over the region which formed the ancient realm of Tonalá. On the east lies the deep canyon of the river Santiago, the formidable barranca which anciently separated the lands of the warlike Chichimecas from the Tonaltecans. It curves northward, cutting a deep course as it passes the dusty village of Huentitán on its way to the town of Tequila. Beyond lie the high, forbidding mountains of northern Jalisco. The double spires of the cathedral of Guadalajara rise in the middle distance, the city spreading in all directions from its colonial nucleus of church, square, and government palace. The part of the city nearest Tonalá was formerly the old village of San Andrés and now consists of working-class dwellings and small industrial shops. A few rolling hills and the hamlets of San Gaspar and El

Rosario separate Tonalá, the capital of the ancient kingdom, and Guadalajara, the capital of the modern state.

Four centuries ago Tonalá headed the region which encompasses the whole plain; at present it is the *cabecera* (head town) of a humble municipality within the state of which Guadalajara is the capital. In the formal structure Tonalá has many ties with the city: its municipal officers are directly responsible to state officials who work in the capital; its budget must be approved by a committee of the state chamber of deputies; town improvements and public health services come under the direction of Guadalajara agencies; and its criminals are tried in the city by laws written by the state legislature. In the highly centralized governmental structure of Mexico the power to make decisions affecting towns and villages is held in offices in state capitals and in Mexico City. But in fact, the influences of the city in this realm are few, for few decisions are made. Most municipal budgets are small (6,000 pesos, equivalent to U.S. $480, was the 1960 budget for the municipality of Tonalá, for instance)—so small that the amount of building, improvements, services, and law enforcement is limited. Since there is little financial support from the national and state capitals, there is little administrative influence.

There are likewise in Tonalá no state-administered educational or welfare programs and no hospital; and until 1963 there was no clinic or public health worker. Villagers desiring these services must go to the city, but most prefer to do without.

In addition to the control exercised by the state government and federal officials, there are six extra-Tonaltecan governmental institutions that influence life in the village: (1) the water agency, (2) the federal school system, (3) the malarial mosquito eradication agency, (4) the national and regional *ejido* (communal land) organization, and (5) the judge of the state Court of First Instance. A sixth agency, the health center, was established in 1963. The first four of these agencies derive their power from the federal government whereas the fifth is an arm of the government of the state of Jalisco.

The water agency is the most important to the villagers. The town water system is administered by a local *Junta de Aguas* (Water Committee) consisting of elected officers plus the local federal tax collector who represents the federal government. The committee works under the jurisdiction of the Guadalajara office of *Recursos Hidráulicos* (Water Resources, a cabinet-rank department). Although the Junta is charged with the maintenance of the present water system, of late its most important job has been to try to collect money owed, so that it can maintain the system. When it exerted pressure in order to collect delinquent bills of as much as three years, it was paid by a minority while the majority grumbled, and on Easter Sunday in 1960 Judas figures bearing the names of four members of the Water Committee and the municipal president were burned in effigy in the plaza.

The Tonalá elementary school is a part of the federal school system. Again administration is centralized so that appointments are made, policy set, and textbooks chosen through the district office in Guadalajara. There is little local autonomy in these matters: for example, in spite of opposition to the teaching of anatomy, there are no ways in which the curriculum can be modified. Local opinion determines policy only on peripheral matters such as whether volleyball should or should not be taught to girls, or whether folk dancing should be included as part of the athletic program.

The financial support of the federal agency is limited.

Although it provides the funds with which the teachers are paid, the village is left the task of maintaining the school plant, a building which in pre-Revolutionary days was a monastery. To the village is also left the task of providing desks, blackboards, and improvements to the school building. However, the village is unable to organize itself to raise necessary funds, so the building is not improved, and the pupils sit on crates or on the floor.

The organization attempting to eradicate malaria is formed through the cooperation of the national government of Mexico and the World Health Organization. Tonalá is one of the towns in the region for which it was decided that the incidence of malaria was high enough so that it is advisable to spray dwellings every six months. Thus, though the Tonaltecan is more aware of the existence of the campaign than the city people, often he is less informed as to the purpose of spraying. There are constant complaints that the insecticide kills cats, but not rats, or that it is ineffective against flies. The complaints continue even though explanatory leaflets are given out (which usually are not read), and the men who do the spraying are trained so that they can answer questions (which are not asked, for the Tonaltecan way is to submit silently, even if resentfully).

The fourth governmental influence from the city comes through the ejido (cf. chap. 9). When the haciendas around Tonalá were divided in 1927, two ejidos were formed, one for the western half of town, and one for the eastern. Because of the administrative structure set up by the land laws, ejidos are operated directly under the jurisdiction of the federal government. In theory *ejidatarios* (members of ejidos) are rural police officers owing allegiance directly to the Department of Agriculture and the President of the Republic. Tonaltecan ejidatarios, however, are not very sure of the existence of this direct line of communication, while the majority of the villagers would have rejected it, even if they had known it existed, just as most of them rejected any participation in the ejido program. At the time the ejidos were formed, most Tonaltecans preferred to reinforce their alliance with the Church rather than with the government, which, they were convinced, was atheistic and permeated by agents of the devil. Consequently, comparatively few Tonaltecans participated in the ejido program, and those who did were without the support of their fellow villagers. The more conservative people felt that the ejido land had been stolen from the *hacendados* (owners of haciendas), the rightful owners. In time the ejido organization from the western part of town disintegrated. Some of its lands are now sharecropped or rented for pasture, while most of its lands, barren and unwatered, lie fallow.

The connection between the existing ejido and the federal government is weak. The ejido seldom seeks the help and advice of the regional office of the Ministry of Agriculture and the Agrarian Department, the two federal agencies charged with the supervision of ejidos. These agencies, in turn, have little interest in the semimoribund ejido of Tonalá, but an occasional effort is made to reach the farmers of the village. Once during my year in Tonalá the agricultural engineer attached to the Guadalajara office of the Ministry of Agriculture showed two educational films—one on soil erosion, the other on the use of fertilizers. Although the showing was open to the general public, few villagers came and fewer yet stayed to watch pictures without the horses, charros, and shooting that delight them in commercial films.

With the help of the school director the engineer organized a club among the youth of the village, the Club

Juvenil Rural, which undertook a chicken-raising project. By the summer of 1960 the club had a membership of twenty, and the engineer had plans for starting projects in carpentry, truck farming, and metalwork. One Tonaltecan boy had been selected to visit the agricultural college in Chapingo (near Mexico City) in the hope of awakening the club members' interest in scientific agriculture. Perhaps by working through the youth of the village, the agricultural engineer can strengthen the tie between the Ministry of Agriculture and the farmers.

The fifth governmental influence from the city is an office of the state of Jalisco, rather than an arm of the federal government. The *juez de primera instancia* (judge of the Court of First Instance) holds a post in the state court system and is appointed to his Tonalá post from Guadalajara. He commutes from the city daily. Both to himself and to the townspeople he is an outsider, for he is a lawyer and a middle-class professional who finds himself among a group of "Indians." They, in turn, understand little of the legal technicalities he is concerned with and consider the state government, which he represents, a body of self-serving politicians. Consequently, they have less recourse to the court system than villagers in communities with elected municipal judges, preferring rather to go to the priest for help in settling disputes and collecting debts.

The health clinic is a new agency in town, established in 1963 when the Department of Health of the federal government instituted a widespread system of clinics and hospitals in Jalisco. The hierarchy of agencies founded includes hospitals and research centers as well as municipal and village health and education centers of the kind set up in Tonalá. Here a nurse gives instruction in child care, diet, and hygiene, administers immunization programs, treats simple ailments and refers more serious matters to an out-patient clinic in Guadalajara. A visiting teacher also gives sewing lessons, and sewing machines and work space are provided for the women who wish to participate.

If one takes these outside governmental influences as they impinge on the average Tonaltecan, the total effect is as follows. From the outside comes a pittance with which the police are paid, a few city teachers and the salaries for those who live locally, an occasional engineer to consult with the Junta de Aguas and demand immediate payment of delinquent bills, a nurse to give immunization shots to children and health lectures to women, another engineer to show movies or talk to some young people, and a few khaki-clad insect sprayers in a yellow jeep. Out of the town go the money paid every month by the water subscribers and the revenues from the licenses, fees, and taxes collected by the representatives of the state and federal offices of Hacienda.

Guadalajara as a center of governmental activity is less important to the Tonaltecan than Guadalajara as an ecclesiastical center. This city is the place of residence of Mexico's only cardinal, and to the religious Catholics of Tonalá this fact makes it the moral and spiritual capital of the country as contrasted with Mexico City, the secular and governmental capital of the nation. Guadalajara is also the seat of the bishop of the diocese to which the parish of Tonalá belongs. The bishop makes at least one annual visit to Tonalá, when he confirms the children of the village. Decisions reached in the city as to the policy and personnel of the church in Tonalá have direct effects in the village. Matters like the degree of cooperation between school and church, the attitude to be taken toward the federal census, the particular sins and omissions to be stressed in sermons, and the elements of ritual to be discouraged as heathen practices are considered by the bishop. Such decisions are of daily concern to Tonaltecans, who listen attentively to the admonitions of the priest, even when they do not follow them.

In addition *Hoja Parroquial,* the weekly parochial newssheet, provides a means of communication from the city to the village. This sheet, which is distributed every Sunday, contains a brief lesson on a text in concordance with the religious calendar, a sermon on the way of life and duties of a Christian, and a half-page of paid announcements giving the thanks of individuals to the saints through whose intervention favors have been obtained. It represents the most widely distributed piece of reading matter in town. In most households it is the only printed material read regularly. Nevertheless, its influence should not be overemphasized, for it is difficult to tell when tacit assent becomes a guide for action; in the year I spent in Tonalá, for instance, no Tonaltecan paid for an advertisement in the *Hoja Parroquial.*

The economic life of the city exerts a more obvious influence upon the village. Guadalajara is the place one goes to buy anything beyond the simple necessities of matches, kerosene, huaraches, and food. Even though a total inventory of a Tonalá house would not make a large or elaborate list, almost everyone must depend upon the city as a source of goods at some points in his life. The long satin christening robes for infants still used in Tonalá baptisms are bought by the godparents in Guadalajara; boys' suits for first communion and the missals carried by little girls are acquired in the city; wedding veils, the suit and shoes for the groom, and the bride's flowers must all be obtained there; and coffins, no longer made in Tonalá, are purchased from Guadalajara funeral suppliers.

Even everyday life may demand trips to city stores. Materials and buttons for dresses must be bought there, as must cloth for mops and for napkins to hold tortillas. Schoolbooks, comic books, and any newspaper besides the one Guadalajara newspaper with distribution in Tonalá can only be obtained in the city. The list is long of things one cannot buy in Tonalá: balls, scooters, and dolls; kerosene stoves, irons, and radios; plates, spoons, hammers, hatchets, nails, boards, *petates* (rush mats), *metates* (grinding-stone used to grind corn for tortillas), *molcajetes* (mortars). Some of these items are the kinds of things one can do without, but others such as simple tools and rush mats, are things that every Tonaltecan household requires for its maintenance.

Tonalá, like many of the towns and villages surrounding Guadalajara, has become dependent upon the city for both necessities and luxuries. This is partly because there are more demands than previously, when, for instance, no Tonaltecan boy could even dream of owning a scooter, and partly because the markup on some items in village stores is so great that people prefer going to the city to buy them. A few Tonaltecans have even taken to buying beans and corn in Guadalajara. Nevertheless, the Tonalá retail stores are still doing a profitable business in staples, for they are closer and offer credit. The owners of these stores buy their supplies on the retail market in Guadalajara; town storekeepers do not buy directly from wholesalers, for they do not purchase in large enough quantities. City wholesalers do not employ outside salesmen to communicate with retail stores or rural buyers.

Guadalajara is a source of services as well as goods. There is no resident doctor in the town, although three city doctors hold more or less regular office hours in Tonalá. Two or three families take their children to a pediatric clinic in Guadalajara, and several storekeepers' wives have had their babies in Guadalajara maternity hospitals. Most Tonaltecans, however, get along with the services of the visiting doctors, the resident midwives, the women who give injections, the curers, and the practitioners of magic. Although villagers do not have regular dental checkups nor do they worry about straightening crooked teeth, sometimes the pain of frequent and severe toothaches drives them to a city dentist. Dentures are more common than popular notions about Mexican teeth would lead one to expect.

Many city services are of little importance to the townspeople. They do not patronize beauty salons, custom designers, travel agencies, art galleries, or libraries. Most of them have no need for the services of automobile mechanics, appliance repairmen, or bookkeepers. Often a feeling of shyness or inferiority prevents their taking advantage of those urban services which might be available and useful to them: in selling land or negotiating a loan, they refrain from seeking the legal advice which could rescue them from the hands of loan sharks or maneuvering city politicians.

Some Tonaltecans earn their livelihood in the city. According to my field census, 194 villagers worked in the city in the spring of 1960. They represent about 20 per cent of the adult male population (1,019 males between 19 and 64 years of age) and 3½ per cent of the total population of the village (5,428). Although some of the urban workers are employed in the neighboring town of Tlaquepaque in pottery factories, most are unskilled factory workers, foundry workers, blacksmiths, automobile mechanics, and lathe operators. The more prosperous families around the plaza send office workers, accountants, and businessmen to the city, even in one case a young man who works for one of the two main newspapers. The transportation industry is represented by seven bus drivers and one bus conductor.

These workers commute daily by local bus, for service is rapid and inexpensive, although not luxurious. Bus transportation is an important lifeline for the maintenance of economic, social, and political integration of town and city. Loaded buses, spaced fifteen minutes apart, shuttling back and forth, bear smoky and noisy evidence of this fact.

The location of the bus route is a clue to the Tonaltecan's Guadalajara. Government offices, department stores, hotels, and middle- and upper-class homes occupy the uptown or west half of the city, but east of the broad Calzada de Independencia lies the lower half of town. Early historical sources refer to this eastern section around the Church of San Juan de Dios as a *pueblucho* (a term approximately meaning a miserable, broken-down village). In time the pueblucho became populous, but it always kept its less prosperous, less substantial economic status. Today it is a mixture of the small homes of the urban working class, tenements, the typical stores of the "low-rent district," cheap hotels, small factories, and repair shops. As in the past, it is here one finds the demi-monde: the houses of prostitution, the cantinas with upstairs rooms, abortion mills, marihuana, and cheap tequila. The last twenty years have added a borrowed trait: large, neon-lighted night clubs offer their excitements of stripteasers, almost-nude mambo dancers, and B-girls.

This is the area the Tonaltecan sees when he comes to the city. His shopping is done in the stands in the Mercado Libertad, in the small shops around it, and in the holes-in-the-wall behind the orphanage. If he works in the city, he is more likely to be employed in factories and sweatshops here than in the elegant stores and offices of uptown

Guadalajara. When he returns from the United States, having worked a few months as a bracero, he spends his money on a prolonged binge in the cantinas. One Sunday sermon in Tonalá was enlivened by a reference to one of these places. The priest commented that Tonaltecan men were spending too much time in the city bars; he was particularly shocked by the name of one called the *Infiernazo* (the large inferno). "In my time," he said, "we thought of the Glory; now you think only of the Inferno."

The villager seldom ventures uptown. Although he knows the shopkeepers around San Juan de Dios often take advantage of him, he finds the uptown stores alien and frightening. His slow, rustic speech and his country-style clothing make him conspicuous. At best, clerks treat him with an impersonal formality he sees as coldness; at worst, he is looked on with contempt as an Indian and a country bumpkin. The Guadalajaran treats the villager with little respect. The city man has little patience with his awkwardness in the urban world, or with his timidity in dealing with officials, his ignorance of the ways of the modern business world of banks and credit. The town he comes from is only a name on the front of the bus to many; to others it is a backward Indian village full of potters.

Some city people know the town from visits. They come to buy cooking utensils and clay curiosities, but their attitude toward the potters is patronizing. "Son algo curiosos para hacer cosas de barro, esos indios" ("They are rather handy at making clay things, those Indians"), is the most common remark made by the visiting city dweller. It is usually made in the presence of the Tonaltecan and always carries the connotion that making clay things is neither important nor suitable work for civilized people.

One day a school bus brought a group of young city

ladies from a private school on a "field trip." They visited the church, walked around the plaza in their starched, blue and white uniforms, snapping pictures of "quaint Indians" and the burros in the street. The visit was in some ways symbolic of the social distance between the city and the town.

Although the town has close economic ties with Guadalajara, entrepreneurs in the city do not consider it as a possible area for development. The city businessman assumes that Tonalá is a poor place to make an investment. In his view the Tonaltecan income is not sufficiently high to provide a good market for goods, not enough capital exists in the town for any kind of community input, and its inhabitants do not understand the "modern" way of life well enough to make the setting up of a department store, a bank, or a service agency feasible. In part they are right. A man from Tlaquepaque established a repair shop for small electrical appliances, believing there were enough radios and electric irons in the town to assure success. Business proved very slow, however, and in 1960 the repair agency was slowly becoming a warehouse for one of the pottery middlemen.

Tonalá is considered a suitable place for another kind of development, however. A couple of years ago a factory producing men's shirts was moved from Guadalajara to the town. By this move the owner gained several advantages: labor costs were lowered, and the negligible municipal taxes represented significant savings. Labor union and social security supervision problems were avoided as well.

The factory employs from forty to fifty people, most of them Tonaltecans, although all supervisory personnel commute from the city. The factory operates in two shifts, and work is organized on an industrial assembly line.

Women employees, paid on a piecework basis, average from sixty to seventy-five pesos a week, while housewives who take work home earn considerably less. By Tonalá standards the wages are high, but by Guadalajara standards the factory is a sweatshop that can exist because there is no governmental interference or supervision in Tonalá. Nevertheless the manager is afraid that state officials may investigate wages and taxes, and he keeps the factory doors locked and his operations as secret as possible.

The factory is important as a portent of future developments. Since Tonalá offers owners of small industries cheap labor, low taxes, and a governmental "free zone" in the proximity of the city, it is likely that more such factories will be established. Similar developments have occurred in nearby Tlaquepaque, and have converted it from a weaving village to an industrial slum. The sweatshop is likely to be a major route whereby the economic influence of industrial Guadalajara spreads to Tonalá.

As yet, however, the Tonaltecans employed in the clothing factory see their relationship to their employer in traditional terms of patron and client. The employees organized a name-day celebration for their owner-patron, including a special Mass in the factory. The owner, for his part, occasionally finds himself lending money to an employee or becoming a godparent to his child, because his workers force him into the traditional role of patron. This pattern is reinforced by the fact that since most employers enjoy the deference and respect that is accorded to the patron, they are willing to play the role to the hilt. Thus, in a small way, Tonalá has affected the operations of the factory.

The factory has brought something new to the town—wage labor for women. As yet many fathers and husbands forbid their female relatives to work outside the home, but inroads have been made. Already some say that it is within the bounds of modesty and honor for a respectable woman to work in the factory so long as she does not become a labor union member. This is a sentiment agreeable to the owner, of course, and he has used it to his own advantage. When one of the city unions attempted to organize the women, the employer convinced them that union membership made marching in patriotic parades mandatory. The thought of women turning out for ceremonies in honor of Benito Juárez, an atheist, a villain, if not a manifestation of the Antichrist for the devout Tonaltecan, was sufficient to kill off any pro-union sentiment.

The factory has also brought along those other items of industrial culture: the assembly line, job specialization (cutters, stitchers, finishers, thread-tiers), and the speedup, although this last practice is only dimly perceived by the villagers. However, the principal observers of the industrial process are women, of little prestige in their households and in no position to innovate in the family's pottery production. Consequently, although pottery-making would lend itself to mass production techniques, potters have not taken up the assembly line or any form of the rationalization of the work process. Even the pottery factory is organized in terms of traditional tasks rather than manufacturing processes.

In other ways the factory is an island in the village. It contributes little to municipal income; to the villagers it offers only unskilled employment; it sells nothing locally. Since the owner feels no civic responsibility toward the village, he does not participate in Tonalá's public affairs. From the standpoint of the town the total economic input consists of the wages paid the employees, for the factory is a Guadalajara enterprise making a city product for the city market.

At first glance factories of this kind would seem to be one of the routes whereby urban culture traits and the patterns of industrial society are carried over to the rural population. However, they do so only in a restricted sense, in that the number of wage earners is multiplied while the number of workers in family production units decreases. In the long run this transformation will have a revolutionary effect on local economic and social structure, if generalizations drawn from studies of the industrialization process in Europe hold true for other parts of the world. In the short run, however, this "sweatshop stage" of industrialization brings few of the benefits of twentieth-century society to villagers, while it puts their income under the control of an "outsider." The outskirts of Guadalajara at present consist of just such enclaves of essentially rural populations working in industry and living in densely settled areas.

The city is, of course, indispensable for the continued existence of Tonalá—even though the formal institutions of the government, the offices of the state and the republic, have limited influence on life in the village. The village is economically dependent upon Guadalajara, bound intimately to the market of the city, drawing financial support from it in the form of wages paid to its residents. But proximity to an industrial center and dependence upon it do not provide automatic avenues for the diffusion of traits and ideas nor for their acceptance. Tonalá can remain in its old ways, ignored by urban administrator and citizen alike.

IV. THE PLACE WE LIVE IN

IF ONE CONSIDERS Tonalá on the basis of size of population alone, it is a town, not a village; for in ancient Mesopotamia, Bronze Age Spain, or present-day Scandinavia it would be populous enough to be classified as an urban rather than a rural settlement. The 1950 Federal Census of Mexico lists it as a *villa* (town) with a population of 3,631, somewhat unevenly divided between 1,778 men and 1,853 women. My 1960 census yielded a figure of 4,886 persons, in 861 of the 1,008 buildings bearing house numbers assigned by the municipality. Since some of the numbered "houses" include places of business, vacant dwellings, and corrals for animals, I assume my count represents about 90 per cent of the population. Assuming that the composition of the uncounted households is similar to that of the houses for which we have information, the projected total would be 5,428. If numbers were all, Tonalá would indeed be a town.

If, on the other hand, one considers Tonalá in the context of the urban and rural culture of Jalisco, of how it is classed by its neighbors, it is a very large village. Its inhabitants earn a living in pottery-making and agriculture. Its streets are cobbled or unpaved, its market is held in the open air, its houses are unplastered and unpainted, and it lacks the urban services of sufficient running water, garbage collection, and sewers. But most significant of all is the fact that its inhabitants are "Indians," both to themselves and to outsiders, a racial minority possessing an "impoverished culture." Tonalá remains a *pueblo* regardless of the census figures.

A map of the town looks as if it had been drawn by Servius Tullius, the Etruscan king who divided Rome into four quarters or wards, for it is neatly cut into four barrios. A second Mediterranean trait is soon evident to the casual stroller of its streets: the *cardo maximo* divides Tonalá into eastern and western halves as it runs from the northern hill to the cornfield on the south, the *decumanus maximus,* running east to west, further divides the town into four *cuarteles* (quarters or wards). The parochial church is given the "place of honor" required by the Spanish Crown in colonial towns. The market, the *presidencia municipal,* and the more important stores are located just off the exact center where the two axes meet. As in Stanislawski's Michoacán towns of Spanish-American tradition (Stanislawski, 1950), the *mesón* (inn) is situated near the church or, in this case what was church property until after the Revolution of 1917. The cuartel division is made more obvious by the street-naming system. As each street crosses one of the axes, its name changes, giving each cuartel a unique set of street names. In other respects, the quarters are not obvious to outsiders; the buildings are much the same in all the cuarteles, there are no signs visible to the casual visitor of occupational barrios or streets of specialized craftsmen, and except for the area around the plaza there is no division into business and residential sections. To local people the cuarteles do differ from each other. Members of one will see those of each of the others as having certain distinct characteristics, describing them as quarrelsome, rough-speaking, freeloading, overly pious, or *mal educados* (badly brought up, vulgar, disrespectful).

The center of town has a certain stamp of its own, as is common in towns set up by the Spaniards according to the grid plan. It is the center of the commercial life of the community, for it is here that the biweekly markets take place, and it is here that perishable foodstuffs are sold daily; it is also here that the more imposing shops are situated and that Tonaltecans buy such necessities as sugar, salt, and coffee for their families, and glaze and pigments for their pottery. Here in the plaza the Sunday evening *serenatas* (band concert and promenade) provide the spice and sweetening of the week's activities. Here are the houses of Tonalá's most solid citizens and its important buildings—movie theater, market, jail, registry—and gathering-place of the political coterie. It is the place with the most *movimiento,* the townspeople say, but the word means more than movement alone; it also signifies noise, people, and color—all things which are valued in the social side of Tonalá life.

The area around the plaza is also more densely populated than the blocks around the edge of town. High value is placed on being in the center of movimiento, not only as a site for shops and businesses, but also for one's home. In contrast to our flight to the suburbs, the Tonaltecan wants to be where "life" is. There are, therefore, no vacant buildings around the plaza and no empty *solares* (house lots). One can picture the population flowing slowly, constantly, toward the center of town and shrinking from the peripheries, so that even though there are more people now in Tonalá than at any time since the Conquest, the boundaries are growing tighter. To both east and west lie fields which were formerly house lots.

The major contrast with the plaza is the *orilla* (edge of town), and villagers make a distinction between *los de la plaza* (those of the plaza)—substantial citizens, the burghers, the men of commerce—and *los de la orilla*—the outsiders, the gatherers and scavengers, the Tonaltecan marginal men. Although the major sector of the population does not fall clearly in one or the other classification (and indeed, for many Tonaltecans daily life may include only sporadic contacts with the plaza and its inhabitants), they hold firmly to the view that sociometrically and stratigraphically the plaza stands for more money, more people, and more movimiento.

The population of Tonalá is spread unevenly over an area about one kilometer square. Much of the area (outside the high-density plaza region) is earthen-floored patio, cornfields, pigpens, corrals, and ponds (wet or dry depending on season). There is so little sheltered area in some blocks that a nineteenth-century reformer would be horrified, but such crowding indoors takes place only during sleeping hours and rainstorms. Most of one's life is spent outdoors. Indeed one is struck with the fact that our dichotomy of "inside" and "outside" is not really applicable there. Although dichotomies referring to the area in which one lives do exist, they are other than ours, so that when writing in English one is pushed into using terms which are awkward and often nondistinguishing.

The geography of the Tonaltecan house bears some discussion.

Certain minimal elements are considered necessary for a house; they are in a sense the defining elements of a human dwelling, and although there are dwellings which lack one or several of these features, houses which fit the description are both the most numerous kind and the Tonaltecan model of what a house is.

Along the edge of the sidewalk the front wall of the house marks the adobe boundary of the inside and outside world. Although a window may open out from the house so its inhabitants can see what goes on in the street, or the wall may be broken only by a door or a simple gap in the adobe from which it is made, or the wall may simply be indicated by a few courses of adobe brick, this is a major division of living space as it is culturally defined.

Beyond the front wall is the outside world into which the men of the family travel and through which they roam. It is a world that is threatening in many ways—inhabited by *aires* which are spirits and swept by *aires* which are winds, the place of temptations for women and possible violence for men. The slightest breeze outside the front door is considered more dangerous than a dust-swirling whirlwind in an open patio. To go out the front door is to be *en la calle* (in the street) with many of the overtones that literal translation into English would indicate. One is en la calle even if off on an errand or at the market or visiting in a friend's house. It is understood that men can and must spend much of their time there either on business or pleasure, but women are expected to avoid going out as much as possible. Not all of them do, of course; for many of them gossiping with friends and neighbors is their main form of recreation, but being seen chatting in the street for any length of time is not highly thought of. To do so very often is to court the risk of getting a name as a town busybody.

There are times, of course, when rules are slackened a bit. Young girls, except for those from the most conservative families, are allowed out in groups for the Sunday evening serenata. Holidays are also a time when it is considered permissible for the women to sit in the plaza and watch the goings-on, particularly if they have the excuse that they brought the little children in for the fiesta. On warm evenings or on Sunday afternoons one can often see family groups, men and women together, sitting in front of their doors enjoying their leisure. This kind of activity does not lead to anything like a block party, however; each family group remains separate even though there is joking and calling back and forth to other similar groups. Often the doorway groups are composed of women and small children only, for many men prefer gathering at street corners or in grocery stores where tequila is sold secretly. The groups of men as contrasted with the groups of women are roughly divided into age-grades, since the purpose of such gatherings is lighthearted relaxation, and one cannot relax in the presence of such respect-inspiring figures as a father or older brother.

Behind the wall is the protected area, the place where mothers, sisters, wives, and daughters are secure, the stationary end of the compass—to use John Donne's imagery—from which a man ranges forth on the activities appropriate to his sex, but to which he is tied by his dependence upon his family as a source of honor and respect. This view of the relationship of a man to his home is similar to what Pitt-Rivers describes for the village of Alcalá in Spain (Pitt-Rivers, 1954: p. 115). Indeed the similarity is so striking one is tempted to assume that this is a part of the culture of Tonalá which was learned from the Spaniards and learned well.

Inside the front wall of the Tonaltecan house there is usually a room just to the right or left of the entry. This is often *the* room of the house in which all the members sleep; its furnishing, if it has any beyond petates, calendars, and religious pictures, consists of one or two double beds, a chair, and less probably a wardrobe in which to store clothes. Often the juxtaposition of the sleeping room and the opposite house wall forms an entry or narrow passage and in most cases it is covered by a roof. This area is a special place in the house, the *pasillo,* and certain activities are appropriate to it.

In pottery-making families it is the preferred work place for women and children, offering them a place which is technically within the "safe" area behind the front wall, but also allowing them to watch the comings and goings in the street. The men, who have much more freedom of action, choose usually to work in another covered area, the *corredor.* It is the region immediately behind the room and is formed by the extension of the roof to a series of arches or posts. It is the most important living area in the house; if any area is paved or floored, it is likely to be the corredor, for it is the place where guests are entertained. Thus the choice of work area reaffirms the position of the male in the household. Furniture tends to be sparse: a few low chairs, sometimes a table, possibly a flowerpot or two. The pasillo, on the other hand, contains no furniture at all.

The average house also has a lean-to kitchen; its peripheral position in the social life of the home is made visually evident by the fact that it is small, its roof is lower than the rest of the house, and it occupies no regular and fixed position as does the bedroom. The kitchen can be situated almost anywhere along the edges of the yard. Sometimes it exists only as a partially covered area where the rain will not put out the cooking fire, while the cooking pots are stored by being hung on the nearest wall.

The rest of the yard is considered to be within the bounds of the house (*en la casa*) as opposed to en la calle. Ordinarily it is a packed-earth area variously dotted with a kiln, a few flowerpots, a hut to store dry clay, a well, and an enclosure for a pig or two. Seldom is one house lot separated from another with the complete set of high walls one would find in most towns of Spanish-American tradition; indeed most town lots are open in back so that the center of each block is a nondifferentiated area. However, that space is certainly not communally owned or lived upon; it consists of plots of privately owned land, usually demarcated only by traditional boundaries (a rock or a guamúchil tree), and planted in cornfields. The center of the block has other functions as well. Since Tonalá houses do not ordinarily contain privies, one retires to the cornfields for elimination. The large open area also serves as a means of access to the houses of relatives on the same block.

At this point it might be well to make a brief mention of the Tonalá living pattern by blocks. The living arrangements and property ownership of the past fall into the realm of conjectural history, since no town records of years prior to 1936 are extant, and informants are fuzzy and wary about property ownership in general. Nevertheless, one can make a guess or two. An aerial photograph of the town taken in the early nineteen forties shows many house lots occupied by isolated houses where now the entire façade along the street is a solid row of small houses. In many cases such blocks now contain phalanxes of patrilineally related, nuclear families. This fact leads one to the conclusion that upon the marriage of sons the new nuclear families were given a part of the paternal house lot. Informants agree that this process is still going on and that it is one of the solutions to the housing of newly married couples. My census found many instances of this kind of residence pattern. The physical arrangement of Tonalá houses often makes blocks—or at least that part of a block fronting on one street—into solid kinship units consisting of patrilocal extended families. That this is not a recent development can be seen by the fact that the occupants of adjoining houses are sometimes descended from a common ancestor of two generations ago; thus some blocks represent, at least analytically, some kind of minimal lineage unit (see chapter on family for further discussion). This residence pattern helps in part to explain the lack of enclosed house units in a society where, in many other respects, people are suspicious of their neighbors and in which the boundaries enclosing the family unit are crucial to the operation of social relations.

In addition to the above "compound" or "patio" type of patrilocality, there is also found a type of residence closer to the classic kind of patrilocality with which anthropologists are familiar. In these cases newly formed nuclear families may choose to occupy the same household as the husband's parents. The Tonalá version of this household arrangement will be discussed in more detail later.

V. THE POTTER TAKES A WIFE

THE KERNEL of a new social unit—the most important unit in Tonaltecan society, the nuclear family—is formed when a marriage is contracted. Fundamentally there are two ways in which a marriage is made: through bride-stealing (*robo*) or by formal arrangement. Both methods are still in use, although the former is assumed to be a rural custom and consequently has no prestige. People less concerned with status consider a robo equally valid and less expensive. Both the Church in the person of the priest and the government in the person of the *presidente municipal* have opposed the custom. The priest includes robo in his omnibus category of *tonterías de los indios* (Indian foolishness), and the presidentes, assuming that elopement is a form of capture and rape and therefore illegal, have levied fines on the capturing grooms. Neither monetary loss, however, nor priestly disapproval has been effective in eradicating the practice.

The procedure is simple. Both participants and the community have shared expectations as to the order of events. In a few cases the "robo" is a real stealing of a girl who has caught the fancy of a young man, but ordinarily the capture occurs with the consent of the bride-to-be and after a period of courtship. The groom enlists the aid of a few of his friends, his *pandilla* (gang), usually composed of age-mates who were neighborhood playmates in his younger days. His own brother and other males with whom he has respect-relations are not members of this group. The boy has previously ascertained when his "fiancée" will be on an errand alone or when he can find her away from the protection of father and brothers. She is waylaid and carried off; nowadays the vehicle used is usually an automobile, although ranchers from the nearby area of Rancho de Santa Cruz still carry their brides off on horseback. The girl is taken out of town—to another village or to Guadalajara—and stays with the groom for at least one night. The couple then return to Tonalá, and the groom places his bride under the protection of the household of one of his relatives or godparents (occasionally the house of her uncle, aunt, or godparents). This latter step of placing the woman in the house of a "neutral" person is necessary before arrangements can be made for a church wedding. The present priest assumes that as long as both parties are under one roof they are still engaging in sexual intercourse without the sanction of a valid marriage ceremony. So far as the Church is concerned, a valid ceremony means a religious one, even though Mexican law requires the performance of a civil rite to make the contract legally binding.

The groom selects someone to represent his case to the

bride's family. His delegate may be a relative, but no special kinsman is preferred, although ordinarily neither his father nor his brothers are expected to perform this service. Again a certain amount of "neutrality" is expected of the peacemaker. Although a relative may be selected, he is not preferred over a nonrelative who is considered an honorable and upright man.

The go-between is accompanied by friends or acquaintances of the groom, and if possible a *compadre* (co-godparent) of the bride's father is included in the group, for his presence should assure them of a welcome.

The groom does not go along but he provides cigarettes and *aguardiente* (distilled liquor). The peacemaker's arrival with these objects provides the bride's parents with the clue to the nature of the visit. The use of cigarettes and alcohol as a clue informing the participants of the formal ceremonial nature of a social event is common in Mexico (Foster, 1948a: p. 249, Parsons, 1936). Once a visit is opened on this note, the same tone prevails in the kind of language and the choice of social phrases used. The second person formal (*usted*) is used even with intimate friends. Words and phrases reflect an old-time courtesy:

"Won't you do me the favor of sitting down?" says the host.

"It is such pleasure to greet you," says the peacemaker, embracing the father. The members of the peacemaker's party in addressing the father emphasize whatever bonds of real of fictive kinship that exist between them: if he is a first cousin of a grandparent, he may be addressed as *tio* (uncle); if he is a second cousin, he may even be called *primo* (first cousin) rather than *pariente* (relative).

The preliminaries set the stage in several ways. The bottle and the cigarettes inform the father of the nature of the call. The formality of behavior creates an atmosphere of respect between the participants in a situation in which there is likely to be a good deal of antagonistic emotion. Respectful behavior establishes distance between the actors in the scene. It allows the father of the bride to maintain his self-respect while he settles the future of a daughter whose loss of virginity has besmirched his honor. The forms of address used evoke the mutual obligations of kinsmen and thus help set up the lines through which communication can take place. It is clear that the initial period of negotiations in which one smokes, drinks, and exchanges stilted pleasantries is very much a necessary part of the proceedings.

The next stage may be initiated by the host's asking, "To what do I owe the honor of this visit?" Or the peacemaker may broach the subject of the purpose of the call. Once this phrase is pronounced, the tone of the proceedings change. The father is hurt, unhappy—nay, outraged. The groom's representatives try various strategies: the groom is a good but impetuous boy who has seen the error of what he did and is anxious to make amends; the groom's family is honorable and is eager to make things right; the couple have already undergone the civil ceremony and want their parents' blessing before the religious marriage is performed. With great reluctance the father gradually begins to be won over. He may eventually call in his wife to tell her of his decision, but she remains in the background. In a few cases, he may refuse to give his approval to the marriage. The girl may then go ahead with the ceremonies, and the priest may decide to marry her without her father's permission rather than have her "live in sin." But the father usually decides to make the best of a bad situation and take an active part in the *presentación* (presentation) to the priest, a step that must be gone through before the banns are read. Celebrations connected with the church ceremony are very elaborate for arranged marriages, but most frequently brides who have been stolen must be content with the simple civil rite and a brief religious one occurring inconspicuously in the midst of the eight o'clock Mass.

Obtaining a bride by "stealing" is an accepted way of embarking upon a marriage. It is the preferred form when the groom feels that he is unlikely to be able to obtain the approval of his future father-in-law beforehand. He may also decide to run off with his bride to avoid the expenses entailed in the arranged marriage. In the past, when Tonaltecans were warring across the boundaries of the town's four quarters, "bride-stealing" was a form of cross-cuartel raid. A young man would gather together a few friends, and the group would ride off on horseback to capture a girl. The raid was looked on as one way of claiming a victory over another cuartel and also as a means of obtaining a desirable young lady whom one could not arrange to marry through regular channels. Cuartel fighting nowadays tends to take place in the symbolic realm: through competing cuartel-centered festivals and soccer games, but "bride-stealing" most often occurs across cuartel boundaries. It also still carries with it the connotation of being a raid. Certainly the girl's father reacts as if it were, and the groom's relatives respond by going through formal peacemaking proceedings.

The "capturing" form of marriage emphasizes some of the lines of antagonism inherent within the town structure, and, in addition, it dramatizes them in a series of symbolic acts, even in cases where the "stealing" is nominal and by agreement. In the first place, the forms emphasize the traditional roles of man and woman. The male is seen as an active force, as masculine power, while the female is seen as passive, receptive, as not intruding her will, *abne-*

gada (self-sacrificing) in a word. Marriage is symbolized as a joining together of two unlike units, of two people who occupy mutually exclusive roles. It is not dramatized as something entered into by mutual consent. The event is celebrated as aggression, on the one hand, and submission on the other.

Secondly, bride-stealing reinforces the split between two affinal groups. From the beginning of the marriage the man and the woman's relatives are assumed to be in opposition. The negotiations which take place so that the required rites can be performed are not the merging of "two families," but diplomatic proceedings between two opposing groups, who compromise, and enter into a compact, while still maintaining their sovereignty.

Thirdly, this form of marriage re-enacts again the separation of the territorial units of the town. The stealing of a bride from another cuartel binds together the men of one cuartel in opposition to another, while it separates "us" from "them"—those of us who belong together and those whom we fight.

If the girl has not been captured, marriage rites begin with the asking of the hand in marriage, the *pedida* (petition). As in bride-stealing, the prospective groom sends a deputation to represent him in the proceedings with his future father-in-law. Again he is not a member of the party, but chooses men who are considered to be respectable and honored and who can make a claim on the bride's father, sometimes asking the village priest to act as mediator. Villagers expect fathers to be reluctant to allow their girls to marry; indeed many families consider that the most honorable course of action is to keep their daughters at home, for in some ways the honor of the family is tied to the chastity of its women, and chastity is threatened by marriage as well as by premarital sexual relations. The antimarriage point of view was strong enough so that the priest frequently devoted parts of the Sunday sermons to explaining that although the Church esteemed chastity, the road of abstention and asceticism was not the only Christian path. To marry and bear children and to be brought up in the Faith is also a virtuous and honorable life. The reluctance of his parishioners to allow their daughters, and sometimes their sons, to marry has driven the priest to take an active part in matchmaking.

The visit is thought of as primarily men's business, but in some families the mother may be present. In other families she will not appear until the matter is all settled and she is summoned from the back regions of the house. Again there is a ceremony surrounding the visit. The go-between must approach the matter carefully after passing the time of day and going through the usual pleasantries of a *cumplimiento* (formal) call. The parents often have a very good idea of what it is all about, but they must feign ignorance, although they may offer the go-between *una copita* (a little drink)—something they would be unlikely to do on other less formal occasions. The subject is then broached; the identity of the suitor is revealed, and there is some discussion of his kinsmen. The parents may then agree to the marriage, but it is more usual to show reluctance. They may set a *plazo* (term), sometimes a long one of a year or more; but if the suitor is impetuous, a long plazo is not politic, for then the fiancé is likely to steal his bride ahead of time.

The bride's parents also have the right to request an assortment of foodstuffs to be delivered to them as part of the wedding ceremonies. In some cases they may itemize details, demanding so many kilos of meat and corn and so many donkey-loads of firewood for making tortillas. If the groom's family fails to fulfill this part of the contract, the bride's father may refuse to allow her to be taken to the groom's house, even though both civil and religious ceremonies have been completed.

The pedida has a secondary function, aside from its primary and manifest one of obtaining parental permission to marry. It also informs the parents that a courtship relationship exists between their daughter and a particular young man. Until this time, although they may have known about the relationship through gossip and personal observations, Tonalá etiquette and morality demand they ignore its existence. If they openly admit or recognize that the young man is courting their daughter before a formal pedida, they would then be expected to put a stop to the relationship immediately, for no pattern exists for open courtship before the petition stage.

The period of the plazo is a time in which the betrothed woman is in a state of transition from the status of an unmarried woman to a married one, from membership in one household group to another. In a very few families betrothal carried with it the privilege of open visits from the groom-to-be. In most families the social amenities of "respect" are maintained through a formal continuation of the "secret" courtship in the doorway or window of the fiancée, but members of the family cooperate by avoiding the front of the house when the engaged couple are conversing.

The transitional state is validated by another custom. During this period, according to more conservative usages, the young man is expected to provide his fiancée with laundry soap and charcoal. She is to use the soap in learning how to wash clothes and the charcoal to provide fuel for her experiments in cookery. If she becomes ill during this time, her fiancé is expected to pay for medicine because, as one informant put it, "she is not completely of the family of her father any more." These customs are now seldom followed in practice, but are mentioned as part of the traditional pattern. It is clear, nevertheless, that the period of the plazo is seen as one in which the young woman completes the learning of her new role.

Two additional formalities must be gone through before the final wedding ceremony. The second of these is the presentación when the couple appear before the priest to announce their intention of marrying. They are accompanied by their parents and a witness for each—usually, but not necessarily, the godparents. The average villager sees the presentation as a request for the Church's permission to marry, and consequently the priest is able to apply sanctions to enforce what he considers proper Christian behavior. As mentioned before, he refuses to publish the banns if the bride-to-be who has been "stolen" is still in the groom's house. He may also refuse to give permission to a marriage involving a village girl and a young man who is suspected of having been swayed toward Protestantism during a prolonged stay in the United States. Or he may use his considerable influence to wrest permission from a reluctant father for his daughter to marry. In the last few years, following the requirements of Mexican law, the priest has insisted that a valid civil ceremony shall have been performed before the religious one. It is not that he is concerned with the importance of the civil rite. He sees rather that by insisting on the civil ceremony he has the government helping in the constant battle against polygynous arrangements. Since this cooperation between priest and municipality is a recent development, there are many cases in which a villager has one wife by law, one by Church, but in fact he is bigamous.

Not all marriages, of course, are both blessed by Church

and legitimized by state, just as some unions are not validated by any ceremony at all. The incidence of such unions is difficult to establish, for although the Federal Census of 1950 contains information on the number of people in each category, it is unlikely that such figures represent the real state of affairs. However, a comparison between the statistics for Tonalá and its urban neighbors indicates that either Tonaltecans are more likely to follow the rules or that they are more unwilling to admit having broken them. While only 5 per cent of couples in the municipio of Tonalá report that they are living in *unión libre* (free union), in Tlaquepaque 10 per cent do so and in Guadalajara 11 per cent. In Tonalá 82 per cent report having had their marriage legitimized by both religious and civil ceremonies, whereas in Tlaquepaque 75 per cent and in Guadalajara 72 per cent do so.

The unión libre category covers several actual situations. In some cases a couple has formed a stable union without having taken the trouble to go through the expected formalities. In other cases, a man has a legal wife, but maintains one or more "spouses" in unión libre. This household, often referred to as a *casa chica,* can be looked on in some ways as the family of the second wife in a polygynous marriage. In a few households in Tonalá, women who have entered into brief and casual relations with several men and have borne children with different fathers may report that they are living in unión libre.

The first of the formalities is that of the civil ceremony —an act considered by the villager to be of such minor importance that it is marked by few festivities or rituals. The presidente, in his role as *juez* or judge, reads a simple act in the presence of two witnesses, and all participants sign the marriage registry. A few families follow the city custom of a supper after the civil marriage, but the menu is still typically Tonaltecan: tamales or *pozole* (a soup of pork and hominy). The couple are not considered married yet, and the groom has no *de facto* rights over the bride as a consequence of his new legal status.

The traditional wedding involves three days of festivities. On the day preceding the church ceremony, the animals necessary for the wedding feast are killed and there is a gathering at the house of the groom called *las visperas de la boda* (the eve of the wedding). It frequently is a heartfelt farewell to bachelorhood with drinking, music, and a supper made of the more perishable parts of the animals. Sometimes food may be sent from the groom's house to the bride's, but even if this is not done, friends and relatives gather there also. The party at the groom's house may last until dawn, but the bridegroom, who has gone to confession in the afternoon or early evening, cannot eat or drink from midnight on. The party continues nevertheless, for it is a solidarity rite of the young men of the community as well as a farewell to a companion about to enter the status of married man.

Meanwhile the bride has also been to confession, having been escorted to church by the wedding *madrina* (godmother or sponsor). Among the madrina's many duties is this one of accompanying the bride when she leaves the house on the day before the wedding. If the madrina does not do so, the bride cannot leave the house of her own accord, and the wedding cannot proceed.

On the day of the wedding the *padrinos* (godparents, sponsors) are expected to provide an automobile and music to escort the bride to church. If these items are not provided, the parents of the bride may refuse to *entregarla* (deliver her), although there is an increasing tendency to do away with the music but to elaborate the floral decorations on the car.

The wedding padrinos are the baptismal godparents of the groom according to Tonalá ideals, but even if the groom and his father decide on another set of sponsors for the wedding, the baptismal padrino may claim what he calls his *derechos* (rights) to pay for the church expenses at the wedding. In addition to church expenses wedding padrinos pay for the automobiles hired to transport the bridal party to the padrino's house after the ceremony and for the flowers decorating the vehicles. The ceremony is usually performed at the eight o'clock Mass, although more affluent Tonaltecans can choose to spend conspicuously by having a special ceremony at another time.

From the church the wedding party goes first to the house of the padrinos where a meal is served to break the fast and then it moves on to the house of the bride. Until this point her parents (particularly her mother) have taken little active part in the wedding; they may not even have attended the church ceremony. Now the bride comes home, escorted by her girl friends, the groom, and his relatives and friends. They carry large clay vessels filled with wedding food provided by the groom's family: *sopa de arroz,* pork in *mole,* turkey in *pipián* (a sauce made of ground peanuts, squash seeds, and chiles), and beans. The food for the total series of festivities is contributed in part by the members of the groom's kindred and by neighbors in his cuartel. People outside the nuclear family thus ratify and support the contract and the alliance between the bride's and groom's nuclear families, reinforcing their own alliance with the groom's family and providing support in the arrangements made with the bride's kinsmen.

All along the route the townspeople come to their doorways to watch the festive procession, which is brought to a climax and ends in a sham battle. At present this is only enacted during carnival periods, but in the past it was part of the regular proceedings, and in some other towns of the state of Jalisco which share a similar cultural base it continues to be practiced throughout the year (Ramírez Flores, 1960). The wedding party is met at the door of the bride's house by her parents, brother, neighbors, and those who consider themselves partisans of her family. Both groups engage in a sham battle with *cascarones* (egg shells) filled with water, ashes, and perfume as weapons, providing a rare occasion for fun and horseplay between the young men and women. This custom is referred to as an *encuentro de papaki* (meeting of the fathers), preserving in the phrase one of the few vestiges of the Nahuatl that Tonaltecans used until this century. Weddings held during the rest of the year are not enlivened by this burlesque warfare, but nevertheless the procession enters, bearing the gifts of food as if they were visiting emissaries.

While the guests are eating, drinking, and dancing in the bride's home, the wedding padrinos take both sets of parents and the couple off separately. The padrinos take the role of mediators, and calling upon the solemnity of the occasion of marriage, ask the parents to greet each other with a formal embrace. This is a difficult time for many people; it is reported to be a moment of strain, an occasion when both sets of participants must capitulate, a time when fathers weep openly.

On this, the second night of the wedding, the bride returns to the house of the madrina. The partying continues, however, in her absence, and the guests may return to the groom's house for the rest of the night.

On the morning of the third day the bride and a group of her girl friends come to the groom's house to serve *atole blanco* (a traditional drink made from corn) with *panocha* (brown sugar) to those wedding guests who are still around and to wash all the dishes used in the wedding feast. Later during the day every one goes to the house of the bride for the *tornaboda,* a feast given by her relatives. At this time the bride is considered completely *entregada* (delivered) to the groom, and from then on he has rights *in uxorem* over her.

Through all the comings and goings, the talks, the obligations, a series of general themes can be discerned: (1) the bride is "delivered" in a literal sense as if she were a symbol of the validation of an agreement; (2) the contingents and supporters of the bride and of the groom remain separate both symbolically and actually during most of the rites; (3) the full series of steps can be taken only if there are mediators—peacemakers, sponsors, advisers; (4) the contract is not final until the day of the tornaboda, prior to which the treaty or compact can be abrogated at several points in the process.

At various times in the three days' activities it is obvious that the drama proceeds as if the bride does not act of her own accord, but is literally "given" in marriage as a part of a transaction with a larger sphere of reference. She cannot leave the house without her madrina as escort. Her father has the option of not allowing her to be taken out of the house, if the conditions of the traditional contract have not been fulfilled (e.g., if she is not provided with transportation to the church)—in extreme cases even when she has already been married by both Church and state. The religious service, of course, underscores the same theme in having an adult male "give her away." Finally, the service which she performs on the third day for her husband's family, and the tornaboda, symbolize and validate the final act of her passage from one family group to another. It is for this reason that consummation of the marriage must wait until after the third day.

The delivery of the bride is accomplished without the

merging of the two families at any point in the proceedings except for the embrace, which, as it were, ratifies the compact between the two sets of parents. Although during most of the three days the groups do not even see each other, the contract can be formed and made binding because the traveling back and forth from one to another gives formal recognition to the importance of both units. In addition, the gifts of food sent from the groom's house acknowledge the debt owed the bride's family, while fitting into the Tonaltecan view of the nature of social relations and the tying of bonds of gift-giving. Again, as in bride-stealing, the ceremonies resemble diplomatic proceedings between two sovereign and distinct units. Direct communication can take place only with the help of a mediator; often it could not take place at all without the tact and manipulations of a practiced diplomat, for the affinal groups are expected to be not only distant but openly hostile as well. Thus the role of padrinos extends beyond that of being witnesses and sponsors in the religious ceremonial to providing the necessary link between the kinship groups which are involved in the marriage.

Thus with three days of ceremonies in arranged marriages—or formal peacemaking followed by civil and religious ritual in bride-stealing—the individuals are moved from one status to another and existing social bonds are reinterpreted. The bride has become wife; the groom has become husband. Both sets of parents are now *suegros* to their son- or daughter-in-law and must recognize a bond which in the past they were expected to ignore. In addition, the two sets of parents are now *consuegros,* a tacit, if distant recognition of their common position relative to future grandchildren.

The ceremonial of forming a marriage alliance shares with that of forming a political one a common narrative, a common set of specific events. It does not necessarily, however, create the same kind of bond. Whereas an alliance by marriage may give a passport into enemy territory and add new people to the category of those from whom one may hope to get (without being assured of getting) support and aid, the same alliance defines opponents without providing machinery for evoking solidarity. Although membership in a cuartel is exclusive—no one can be both a member and a nonmember, or be a member of more than one unit—no one speaks for the cuartel. No one is its collective representative; no one has formed an alliance on its behalf. Consequently the bonds formed by a marriage alliance are, after the wedding, binding only on the husband and wife; for everyone else their maintenance depends on repeated validations, on the choice to make active what is a latent contract. The diplomatic proceedings have produced a safe-conduct and a temporary armistice.

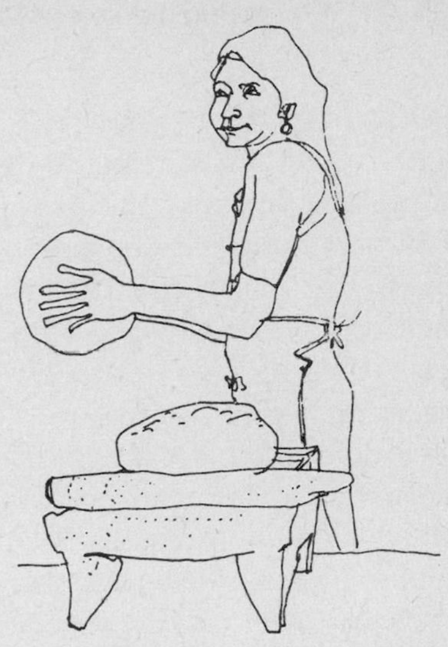

VI. WITHIN THE WALLS OF THE HOUSE

According to village tradition a newly married couple is expected to live with the groom's family. The bride is to take her personal possessions—her clothes, a few doilies and cloths for wrapping tortillas, the earrings and ribbons which are considered necessary feminine accouterments—and come to live and work in a different household. Informants agree that this is the Tonalá way of doing things, even though many of them know that city people set up new independent households when they marry. Many villagers feel that this is another custom which marks them as Indian and unprogressive, even "less civilized," according to some.

A first look at the census material seemed to indicate that not only was there some discrepancy between actual practice and the townspeople's view of their customs, but that the discrepancy was great enough to make one wonder about the informants' grasp of reality.

On the basis of equating each house number with a household, the following results were obtained: 640 households contained only the members of a single nuclear family. In an additional 14 there lived a nuclear family plus "lodgers"—either another nuclear family or a single individual—who were considered unrelated to the head of the household. "Unrelated" in this context probably means that they had no kinship ties closer than second cousin. In six additional households a couple had living with them one or more additional relatives—nieces and nephews, stepchildren, godchildren—so that there would be adults and children in the house. One hundred and four households were clearly three-generation extended families. In seven other cases the old parents had died, and the residence unit consisted of a pair of brothers, their wives, and children. There were twelve houses occupied by unmarried or widowed siblings, usually only a pair, but in one case five brothers and sisters together. Fifty-four households were classified as nonpatrilocal extended families; they were three-generation households and usually included a son-in-law and his children. Thirty Tonaltecans lived alone. In four cases it was impossible to determine the relationship of the household members. Thus, the census revealed an overwhelming preponderance of nuclear family residence units.

The discrepancy between the norm and the customary rule stated by informants was somewhat lessened by the nature of Tonaltecan house arrangements. During my year in the village, house numbers were assigned by an employee of the municipal government. However, since often the architecture of the Tonalá house is somewhat informal, and it was difficult to decide just what should be numbered as a dwelling unit, the final decision was to assign a house number to each exterior door—a logical procedure, but one which does not necessarily reflect the reality of the village living arrangements.

Many Tonalá blocks consist of walls fronting onto the street, but they are hollow in the center; that is, the walls that divide the houses from each other frequently do not run all the way to the back of the house lots and there are no walls across the back of the property. The blocks are large, and the central area is sometimes large enough to be used as cornfields. The open property is not held communally; it is individually owned and worked, but it is not separated into plots by walls or fences. This open arrangement is different from the walled-in houses and corrals of the more "Spanish" towns of Jalisco, but is common among "Indian" towns and villages. The blocks around the plaza, however, where Tonalá's middle class lives, are checkered by high walls and divided into a series of almost impregnable house-forts.

Even when a newly married couple do not settle down with the groom's parents, they prefer to find a house in the groom's cuartel and often near the paternal home. In some cases, a separate room or lean-to is built to provide a hearth and sleeping quarters for the new nuclear family. The new "house" is seldom walled off completely so as to separate it from the dwellings of the rest of the family. Depending upon the placement of the new room on the house lots, it might be given a door to the street or might share a common entrance. In the former case, the domestic unit would appear on the census as a nuclear family; in the latter, as an extended family. In either case, the resulting household arrangement consists of a series of separately roofed rooms and individual hearths or kitchens, which share a joint patio and corral and sometimes a joint entrance.

Unfortunately, I did not obtain detailed information as to the history of the ownership of house lots nor did I trace the changes in occupation of houses over time. It is therefore impossible to account accurately for the development of particular residence patterns revealed by the census. By comparison with an aerial photograph taken in the early 1940's, it seems that former open spaces on house lots have been filled with more buildings, while vestiges of former walls and house lots at the edge of town indicate that Tonalá at some unknown time in the past occupied a greater area. Local tradition supports this view. The same time period has seen an increase in population. One must assume that a tendency toward concentration of population accompanied growth. At present, whole blocks contain patrilineally related relatives: a long, uninterrupted row of Garcías, for instance, along Calle Emiliano Zapata—father, sons, patrilateral cousins, a pair of unmarried, elderly, father's sisters. Other families cluster in a similar manner, if less dramatically, to form loose units that could be called patrifocal. The residence rule and the residence preference are important, not in the sense that they contribute to the development of corporate lineages, but in that they place together a particular complement of role players in daily social interaction.

The basic economic unit is the nuclear family, not the total residence group. The earnings of the members of each family are controlled and dispersed by the father. He has the right to make his own decisions as to the economic contracts he wishes to enter into: to supply pottery, to rent or purchase land, to go as a farm laborer to the United States. In practice, however, he consults his own father.

The presence of the older male in or near the household makes it possible for him to supervise or at least watch over his son more closely. The respect-behavior demanded of sons reinforces the conservative patterns of behavior deriving from the proximity of the father. When there is the possibility of the choice of alternative modes of action, that of the older generation is likely to prevail. Although there may be exceptions, members of the older generation prefer modes of action with which they are familiar, which have been tested and found satisfactory, which will not upset their view as to the nature of things. Consequently, although many of the young men have been to the United States and are acquainted with other ways of life, within the household traditional patterns of action and traditional values are preferred.

The nuclear family is also the basic consumption unit. Each group maintains a separate hearth and cooking area. Each wife purchases her own supplies and is responsible for the washing and mending of the clothes of her husband and children. Nevertheless, the conservative influence of the rest of the extended family is strong in this area also. For a son to set up a house that outshines that of his father would be disrespectful. For him to build a house better than the ones of his relatives in the block would be presumptuous.

A young man's wife cannot insist on changes in standard of living or in household customs without suffering certain penalties. She is an outsider, but she must somehow manage to interact with her mother-in-law and the other women of the family in the close contact of daily life in one patio. This is not an easy position. If she were to insist on having running water installed, she would be sure to run into female opposition. As one woman said to me in discussing her sister-in-law, "Que catrina se ha puesto. Antes estaba muriendo de hambre y ahora es tan fina que no puede ir a la presa a lavar." ("How elegant she has become. Before she was dying of hunger, and now she is too fancy to go to the dam to wash clothes.") Few women are hardy enough to brave the wrath of their in-laws and step out as innovators.

Although the presence of other relatives in the household unit has an influence on the nuclear family's economic activities, the fact that it is supposed to have economic autonomy is nevertheless important. Each nuclear family unit of the household collects, saves, and dispenses its money separately. No one in the extended family can control these separate sums of the separate nuclear families. The extended family does not supply the basis for the formation of capital.

In only a few instances is it the basis for any kind of economic cooperation. Ordinarily an extended family owns only one set of oxen for field work or a burro or horse for transporting goods. It is acknowledged that one member of the group is the real owner, but he is expected to lend his animals to members of his residence group whenever they need them. Only the owner can sell or dispose of the animal. Potters of several nuclear families living in one household fire their wares at the same time, share a single kiln, and buy fuel as a group. Aside from these few activities, presence in a single household does not call for economic cooperation.

The household group consists of a plurality of nuclear families, but it is a single socialization unit. Although an infant's mother has the primary responsibility for his care, he is frequently tended by other relatives. The child's paternal grandmother in particular holds him and comforts him, but babies are fussed over by all the female members of the household. Even the men will try to distract a crying child or will play with a toddler, though they do not take any direct responsibility for feeding or changing diapers. The runabout child has the freedom of the entire patio area. He is not conscious of the divisions of the area into grandmother's house, uncle's house, and his own house. He plays with his siblings and cousins in a yard and corral that is shared by all of them, and although his mother has a separate cooking fire and sometimes a separate kitchen, he may choose to eat with his grandmother or an aunt instead. His father and mother have a separate sleeping room, but he may occasionally or sometimes constantly spend his nights with his grandparents.

In this kind of situation the child is punished or rewarded by almost any elder in the household. He comes to have many mothers. This fact is reflected in the kinship terminology. Although the formal kinship terms are the standard Spanish descriptive terms, in daily usage children may both refer to and address grandmothers as "mother." Women of the older generation who are not "mothers" become "aunts" and men become "uncles." Grandfather may be called *papá,* but less frequently than the grandmother is called *mamá.* There are complications, however. A child calls his father's brother's wife "aunt," but she does not always get by with acting as a lesser "mother" toward him. Co-sisters-in-law have a difficult relationship. Although they are both strangers in their husbands' home, they are not allies. The tension of their position is often expressed in their jealousy of each other, in their taking part in the daily small squabbles between their children at play. Whereas a woman cannot really object to her mother-in-law punishing or rewarding her child, she sees any such action by a co-sister-in-law as either unjust persecution or as alienation of affection.

The household group is tied together as a socialization unit by the close and frequent interaction between alternating generations. Grandparents try to persuade children to sleep in their bed rather than in their parents' room. Grandmothers may prepare favorite dishes for their grandchildren or, as in some homes, routinely take over the task of serving food to some of the children. Older relatives spend evenings or Sunday afternoons telling the household children of the history of the town as they conceive it, folk tales and Christian legends, or moral stories of catastrophes visited on sinners and heretics. In some households grandparental catering to the needs of grandchildren takes on the air of weaning the children from their parents. It is one of the troubles that daughters-in-law complain of to the priest. He is convinced there is truth and justice in the allegation, and occasionally he chastises the the older women for "stealing" their grandchildren from their mothers.

It is within the extended family that the child learns both how to be a villager and how to be a potter or farmer. This fact has some bearing on how he conceives of his economic role. As mentioned below (p. 164), the slow, gradual learning of economic role within the family tends to emphasize traditional modes of behavior. Tradition becomes even more entrenched when teachers are both fathers and grandfathers.

In summary, the structure of the Tonalá household favors the persistence of conservative and traditional norms and activities for a series of reasons:

(1) The presence of the old father in the household influences the economic decisions of the heads of the nuclear families within the group.

(2) The independence of the separate economic units

prevents the formation of large, effective sums of capital.

(3) The fact that the socialization unit is a three-generation extended family emphasizes the conservative aspects of role learning.

VII. IN THE BOSOM OF THE FAMILY

THE IDEAL NUCLEAR FAMILY in Tonalá seems familiar enough. It has overtones of the Roman patripotestal one and of the Irish family described by Arensberg and Kimball. Indeed it seems like the very model of a nuclear bilateral family. Father represents authority while mother is affectionate, warm, and nurturant. The *Hoja Parroquial,* parish religious weekly, contained in one issue a model of what the editor—and probably most of the readers—considered the ideal pattern. Villagers were constantly, almost daily, exhorted by the parish priest to live up to this example. Paraphrasing the writer of the *Hoja Parroquial*:

> The first duty of the father is that he should *be* the chief and head of the family. He is also expected to support the family, to treat his wife with respect and love [the writer's

word order, not mine], to educate his sons in a Christian manner.

The mother, on the other hand, is expected to submit to her husband—unless he is being dishonest. She should be humble and modest. She is the molder of the souls of her children in accordance with Jesus, the divine model. From the time they babble their first words, she should instill in them the love of God and horror of sin, and she should cultivate in them the Christian virtues, principally by the example of a life without stain. As the father's primary duty is to exercise his authority as the head of the family, the mother's is to foster her children's Christian virtues.

The children should respect and love their parents; they should obey quickly, exactly, and with pleasure. Their duties toward their parents should be performed not only during infancy and adolescence but as long as their parents live.

It is then pointed out that Christ lived the major part of his mortal life under his parents' authority. "Oh, sons of the family," says the religious writer, "learn to obey!"

Such are the bare outlines of what the Church and the priest expect of village mothers, fathers, and children. Such is frequently what villagers expect of each other and occasionally of themselves.

An analysis of both the ideal pattern and the daily interactions of nuclear family life reveals certain basic aspects or themes. The nuclear family is conceived of as a series of chains of dyadic relationships. The statuses involved in the dyads are defined on the basis of age and sex, so that each status is unique, and each dyad joins together two statuses of differing authority. There is a split between the authority and responsibility components of power relationships.

The anthropological practice of describing the nuclear family on the basis of the eight logically possible role relationships makes it seem almost necessary that the family model be that of a network of dyads. It is not true, of course, for it is equally possible logically to have patterned alliances in the family involving a triad. Indeed, given the fact that one may frequently have several role players occupying two of the statuses ("son" and "daughter"), subsidiary groups theoretically can be formed in opposition to each other: "men" against "women," brothers against sisters, older generation against younger. The Tonalá family, however, is lacking such solidary groups. Between members of the nuclear family there are reciprocal obligations and expectations, but reciprocity does not imply equality of status. There is no ideology of a "democratic" family with equal votes.

The dyadic model of family relations is reflected in usages connected with referential kinship terms. A brother speaking to his sister will refer to "my father" and "my mother" even though they share the same set of parents. A parent refers to "my son" and "my daughter" even when speaking to his spouse.

The husband-wife relationship can be characterized as that between the *macho,* virile, aggressive male, and the *mujer abnegada,* the self-sacrificing, dutiful woman. But beyond that, the complementary nature of the relationship has religious validation. Its goal is the establishment and maintenance of a good Catholic family in which respect for males and the virginity of the females will be maintained. Although the concept of romantic love is recognized in the town, and shapes the courtship pattern, it is not considered to be of primary importance between husband and wife after marriage. His authority, his ability to command and be obeyed, are essential for the maintenance of his role performance. Her obedience, her service, her sacrifice form the core of her role vis-à-vis her husband. His relationship with her is not characterized by mutuality or trust. From her point of view, what is demanded is formal performance, and in some households she gives no more than this—no affection, no love. In others, the couple has found a mutually satisfying way of striking the balance between male authority and female obedience. In many families, the husband's and wife's common interest in the welfare of their children has molded a marriage of warmth and affection.

However, many Tonaltecan husbands are absent from their homes for long periods of time. A family head may come to the United States to work as a farm laborer or take a pottery-making job in Tijuana, but his absence does not disrupt the working of the family. With a husband gone, the town woman complains of economic difficulties if he does not send money home, but few of them complain of loneliness. The husband has always occupied a distant position, and his absence does not really change the daily life of the family.

The relationship between mother and son has almost a sacred quality. Some observers have noted that the Holy Family is modeled on the human family. Bushnell (1958), for instance, speaks of the Virgin of Guadalupe as surrogate mother. Both poets and social scientists, as well as the writer of the *Hoja Parroquial,* have remarked that the Holy Family provides the Catholic Mexican with a model for family roles and the relationship between them (Paz, 1961: p. 84; Diaz-Guerrero, 1955: p. 415). But whichever direction the influence takes, certain attributes are shared by the Virgin and human mothers as seen by the sons. Mother is the embodiment of self-sacrificing love, a love which is not tinged with the stain of original sin except in the minds of religious theoreticians. The town boy or man mentally separates his mother from the world of sin and sex. Her love for her son is expressed outwardly through her serving him, providing him with food, and by her sacrifice and suffering. A list of those aspects of the Virgin which are venerated in Tonalá illustrates the qualities which are inextricably associated with the mother role: The Virgin of Solitude, Our Lady of Sorrows, Most Holy Mother, La Purísima, Our Lady of Tears. And parallel to the relationship of the Virgin and Christ, often the son unwillingly makes his mother suffer as he assumes the role of the adult male. In order to play out the role of male among males, a young man sometimes enters into activities considered either dangerous or immoral by his mother: he spends time in the billiard parlor, he goes to the city or Tlaquepaque cantinas or houses of prostitution, he drinks, sings, shouts, hires a mariachi to follow him around. He creates an *escándalo* (the overtones here imply noisiness as the primary source of notoriety) to prove himself a man of the real social world around him. In former days he also carried a gun and sometimes got himself shot. Or his "betrayal" may be of another sort. He may choose to seek his fortune by going north to work as an agricultural laborer in the United States or in the developing regions of Sinaloa or Sonora. He may decide to marry in Tonalá and set up his own household, an act which many a Tonaltecan mother interprets as the abandonment of the maternal hearthside. *Se me casó* ("He got married on me" is the underlying meaning) is the phrase with which she tells of a son's marriage. Whatever route he takes, he is faced with a choice of loyalties. This aspect of the mother-son relationship is reflected in the popular culture, and in turn the popular culture reinforces the townspeople's expectations in regard to behavior.

The mother-daughter relationship is marked by other emotions and expressed through a different set of behaviors. Of all the people in the family, mothers and daughters are probably the ones who see the most of each other. Daughters begin learning their economic role at a very early age from their mothers, and there becomes established a high degree of interdependence and a sense of solidarity in reference to work activities. Nevertheless, this, the most intimate relationship in the household so far as work and communication are shared, is marked by an ambivalence not characteristic of the mother-son tie. In some families the daughter becomes the scapegoat on whom the mother can visit her anger at the frustrations of daily life. In a family wherein members are hierarchically ranked, the daughter is often the buck private—until a daughter-in-law moves in. Nevertheless, the mother-daughter relationship is very strong, characterized by mutual dependence and weakened neither by marriage nor time.

Father and son also share some economic activities. In pottery-making households the son learns his craft by imitating his father, in farming he forms part of the work team for plowing, weeding, and harvesting. Yet no anthropologists speak of father-son solidarity in the Mexican family. The son's very close relationship with his mother is construed by the father to be at his expense, so that on another level the two are rivals. Aside from the son's learning his economic role from his father, the major interaction between the two consists of father commanding, the son obeying with outward respect. The alternative is avoidance of each other (see pp. 89–91).

Father and daughter, whom one would expect to have a warm relationship toward each other, do not have many avenues for the expression of their affectionate regard—certainly many less than the mother and son. The father may be indulgent toward the daughter in providing money for new clothes or in buying trinkets. He may escort her proudly to a church bazaar or to the movies, treating her as if she were breakable in her finery of starched, frilly dresses, earrings, and hair ribbons. On these occasions she is to him the young virgin, the dove. But usually his affection for her is hidden by restraint and stiffness. He must keep his position of elevated respect at all times and, consequently, is distant and withdrawn with all family members. He must be especially so with his daughters, for he is the macho, the male; his masculinity is an inherent threat to his daughters. Indeed the only stories of incest that I heard in the village were references to father-daughter relations. The town does not look on such matters lightly, but punishment is usually left to God or supernatural forces.

In one case, the girl's father allegedly forced her to have sexual relations with him. The night this occurred was marked by a fierce storm with high winds, thunder, and lightning—a storm more terrible than anyone remembered for that time of the year, according to the narrator. The girl became pregnant as a result of the rape, and indignation ran high in the town. For a while there was talk of lynching, but no one took the initiative to organize action. The explanation given later was that the father had a relative in the city who was a lawyer, and the townspeople did not want to risk the displeasure of an influential man. No one discussed the possibility of recourse to political authority. Incest is a crime against God and nature, according to the people of Tonalá, and not a government matter. The supernatural forces finally took a hand, and the baby died at birth.

The possibility of father-daughter incest is something the villagers are aware of, and consequently the relationship between the two is marked with constraint and formality. The major interaction consists of the daughter serving the father. She helps wash and iron his clothes; she makes him tortillas; she serves his food; she brings things he asks for, but in the main her area of activity and his are separated.

The relationship between siblings can also be characterized as sets of dyadic relationships. It is difficult to see any behavioral reflection of a solidary sibling group. I cannot once recall anyone using the word "we" to refer to a group of siblings unless the household consisted only of brothers and sisters, in which case "we" was really used in reference to the household itself.

The relationship between cross-sex siblings, like that between father and daughter, is marked by restraint, by the authority of the male vis-à-vis the female, and by the service the sister gives the brother. The brother's authority usually comes into play as he is watchdog over her virtue. He tries to prevent her from talking to men outside the family; he interrupts if she is being courted; he insists that she be chaperoned. The sister, of course, is resentful of these restrictions, even though they are part of the normal expectations of life. If he were less watchful, she would feel he was lacking in proper family feeling. Brother and sister have few common interests, for there is little basis on which to form an alliance.

Even same-sex siblings ordinarily do not form themselves into an alliance in opposition to the older generation. Siblings are not viewed as being equivalent—neither are they treated thus as persons by their parents nor as statuses, for they are distinguished according to age and sex and arranged hierarchically. Each sibling status is unique within the family.

These stereotypes of the social relationships within the family are oversimplifications, of course. There are families with a domineering mother, and there are families with weak fathers or companionable ones, and in these cases, all other family members adjust their role behavior so that the relationships between all pairs are then different from those described above. But the everyday expectations of the townspeople are of autocratic fathers, self-sacrificing mothers, sons obedient to the father, affectionate toward the mother, and virtuous daughters who serve and sacrifice like "little mothers."

The social distance which characterizes the way in which marriages are made, as well as the interrelationships within the family, both derives from and is daily supported by the division of economic roles. By using the criteria of sex and age, economic activities are divided so that there is little overlap between what different persons do. The one possible exception is in pottery-making, but even then, although the definition of male and female roles may differ from one household to another, the separation of tasks in any one family tends to be consistent, clearly understood by all members, and to involve the minimum overlap of functions. For most economic tasks what is done by a woman is not done by a man; what is done by a man is not done by a boy. Boys perform peripheral male activities, while girls perform subordinate female ones. The two criteria and the consequent division of labor provide two themes or ideas about social relationships that are found permeating most social interaction in the village: (1) the sphere of man and the sphere of woman are strictly separate, and (2) statuses are arranged hierarchically by age. In addition, the fact that there is little overlap of activities makes for a rigid system. If the role-player normally assigned to a task is absent, the task may have to go unperformed. If mother is ill or out of the house, no one else can take the responsibility of preparing the meal. In a patrilocal household the problem is solved by eating with one of the other nuclear families, but the general feeling is that no one else can do the job. A death in the family puts great strain on the system of role allocations. Usually a family tries to fill the void with another person to take over the economic role—the father's sister may move in, so she can cook and clean, the mother's brother may take over the head of the household if the sons are not yet grown, or the son-in-law if there are only grown daughters. It is important to have all the family roles filled, for members are dependent upon one another for the maintenance of the family unit.

The family system runs by interdependence and strict role separation. It is integrated on this basis, but such a mode of integration is precarious and threatened by new behavior patterns. Everyone understands what a man does and what a woman does as long as the activities are the traditional ones. As soon as one introduces new activities, one raises the question of whether they are properly masculine or feminine. For many village individuals it is easier to avoid making a decision than to withstand a threat to one's sex identity. New behavior patterns also raise the possibility that paternal authority is threatened.

The third general theme of family organization is that of a split between the locus of power and that of responsibility. In the formal structure the mother is responsible for the actions of the members of the family, but she has no direct power. This creates a situation that is conflict-ridden and frustrating for the mother. There are ways out: social chaos in the household, dependence on the saints, the priests and the Church, and manipulation. All take place, of course, but only the last is of interest here. Through manipulation a role-player—the mother—with little overt authority is able to gain her own ends when she is able to use accepted rules of behavior and role expectations to support her. An example will perhaps make the matter clearer.

Lupita, a young unmarried woman, was telling me how difficult it was to arrange to talk to one's boyfriend, since fathers and brothers object to any courting that they see going on. She had been talking to her boyfriend at the front window of the house when her married brother arrived on the scene. The boy left immediately, but her brother had caught sight of him and was angry. "Who was that here at the window?" he asked.

"No one that concerns you," she snapped back.

"Of course it concerns me," he replied.

"That's only because you don't mind your own business. After all, you are married now, and you are not my boss," she said. But she evidently felt that she was on shaky ground, for she said that she halfway expected him to slap her for her impertinence, but somehow, from somewhere she got the courage to face him.

At this point the father came to the door to find out what the shouting was about. Lupita told him that her brother was being impossible. The brother tried to explain what the fight had been about and ended by saying, "Why don't you keep better watch over your daughters?" The father only shooed them both into the house. Although the brother let the matter drop, Lupita was afraid that the incident would not end there, for she felt that her sister-in-law would needle her brother, who would in turn talk to her father and get him aroused enough to lay down an ultimatum. And her father's ultimatum she would have to obey.

She decided to take a little action of her own. She went to help her mother with supper and started to complain about how her brother's wife would nag him, and he in turn would put pressure on the father. Her mother was a willing listener; she had other scores to settle with her daughter-in-law; for she felt that the younger woman was an interloper who had come between mother and son; she felt that her husband was too sympathetic to the daughter-in-law; and that the daughter-in-law tried to alienate the grandchildren from the grandparents. As soon as the father came to be served his dinner, the mother began to scold him for letting his sons take over his authority and for not wearing the pants in his family. He responded in the way mother and daughter had anticipated. He decided to let the incident drop and went out immediately after dinner, rather than stop to talk to his son.

The incident demonstrates several points: in the first place, a person with little authority (the mother, a person with responsibility but little overt power) was able to achieve her ends; she was willing to maneuver the father, the power-holder, because of her desire to frustrate the daughter-in-law's manipulations; she was able to do so by appealing to the formal structure (namely, the father holds the power, not the daughter-in-law) put in terms of the easily understood cultural symbol of who wears the pants. Note also that the father's decision is dramatized as withdrawal.

Another kind of manipulation relies upon the effective tie between mother and offspring in combination with her overt lack of power in the formal structure. By words, gestures, and mien she transmits the message, "Look how I suffer as a result of your misdeeds." This is a very powerful weapon indeed, for it plays upon the vast buried sea of guilt feelings of the children. As the mother weeps silently, withdraws, refuses to go out of the house, ceases eating, hides her face behind a shielding rebozo, she is engaged in a passive resistance campaign that is quite successful in forcing her children to conform to her wishes. It is a less effective weapon in handling her husband, but it works there sometimes too.

In the incident of Lupita and her family, who was the decision-maker? On the surface everyone is. The father wears the pants and decides not to take direct action. The brother initiates action. The sister-in-law moves the brother to take action (or perhaps it is only the sister's image of her brother's wife that is an actor in the scene). The mother precipitates a decision in the direction she wants it made. The sister gives just the right cues to mother so that things move her way. One is left with the impression that the women are maneuvering busily.

It is also important to note that the women's decision-making is implicit and hidden; since according to the formal structure women do not hold power, enforcing their decisions on others must be done by other means than direct commands. If power is the ability to have others do what you want them to, then manipulation is an alternative mode of behavior in respect to power. The dichotomy of expressive and instrumental leadership when applied to the family is often taken to mean this division between formal and informal leaders, but it is somewhat misleading to see the two sets of terms as coterminous.

For one thing, the informal decision-maker may manipulate the situation and the role-players in order to make decisions concerned with instrumental and adaptive goals —that is, those goals concerned with the relationship of the collectivity, in this case the family, to the outside world; decisions in this adaptive area are made by the instrumental leader (cf. Parsons and Bales, 1955). The fact that a Tonaltecan mother can manipulate the situation in such a way that she decides whether a piece of property should be sold, or what occupation the son should go into, means that there are possible modes of action whereby she becomes the *de facto* instrumental leader. Secondly, since our model ties together mother, expressive leader, and integrative functions, we tend to see her in the leader role as some kind of clucking hen, keeping things calm, peaceful, and running smoothly. Of course, at least part of the time she does this. But part of the time she is also creating conflict and enlarging the social divisions in the household in order to attain other goals—sometimes personal ones, at times other integrative goals that she considers of more importance—somewhat like stopping a prairie fire by building a fire in front of it.

Up until now we have been talking about implicit and unrecognized decision-making. How do things work in reference to explicit authority?

All the members of the family are expected to behave with respect toward the father. This means that a member does not drink in his presence except on ceremonial occasions, that sex, lovers, boyfriends and sweethearts are never mentioned when he is around, that one does not quarrel or fight when he is in the house. Failure to show respect is quickly punished with a slap or a beating depending on the temperament of the particular father and how much face he has lost. Consequently, the social distance of the respect relationship is underscored often by physical distance. Young girls go about their female chores in the kitchen or a corner of the patio; boys soon learn that things are more comfortable when they are out of the house. Except when small boys are busy at specific chores, they spend their days in the street or the plaza. They play away from home; they run in to snatch a bite of food whenever they are hungry. One might label this the phenomenon of the "absent child" in contradistinction to the absent father.

As a result of the need for maintaining distance between the father and other members of his family, daily life is arranged in such a way that there are few occasions for validating group unity through common activities. Meals are not the structured sit-down affairs we are used to; partaking of dinner transmits a kind of message other than togetherness. Rather it is an occasion in which authority is validated in that father is served preferentially vis-à-vis sons, while women serve the men first and themselves afterward. This pattern is quite different from that of the urban middle class where the dining room forms the nucleus of the house, and of the time the family is together, the greatest amount is spent there. Leisure time in Tonalá is likely to be spent in sex-differentiated groups. Women and small children cluster in doorways on warm evenings and gossip and tell stories; men play billiards in the billiard parlors or stand around street corners and talk politics. Even church-going underscores the divisions rather than ceremonially supports family unity, for family members go to church separately, men and women sit on different sides of the church and usually belong to different religious associations.

Since daily life emphasizes the fact that society consists of intermeshing series of relationships between pairs of individuals, the responsibility component of authority, that is, responsibility to a bounded group, tends not to be very obvious.

Within the family the child sees the mother as the responsible person both in daily behavior and in the ideal picture of family relations. Indeed, the structure is such that the responsible person and the power holder are not the same. In the final result, responsibility is seen to be part of female role behavior.

What is seen as the attribute of power and of the male

role, of the father the child wants to be like, is power divorced of responsibility. In all societies, the child probably first learns the authority role in respect to the obvious attributes of his father: he smokes or he can stay up late or he handles the magic flutes, or some other surface behavioral clue. But this view is overlaid by other propositions as the child grows in understanding and adds to his knowledge of what father does: he works, he supports the family, he makes decisions. But if what goes on within the walls of the house is patterned in such a way that the small boy does not see these responsibility attributes of the authority figure in action, he tends to make the equation: authority = power without responsibility. In this instance the father does not undertake actions within the walls of the house; as the person responsible for the nuclear family unit in a larger context, he is completely absent, distant, or removed from what the child is allowed to see. The father's behavior outside the walls of the house is as mysterious to the child as what goes on in a *kiva* for a five-year-old Hopi.

Ideally speaking, the Tonaltecan father is responsible to the government for the actions of his family members and his power over them, and also to the Church. In practice, responsibility toward governmental agencies in this sphere is minimal, for governmental action in reference to family units is well-nigh nonexistent except in large cities. In Tonalá there is no government agency with jurisdiction over matters of family and child welfare except the Court of First Instance, a part of the state judicial system. Few Tonaltecans use the court for suits involving kinsmen; they are thought of as private matters, not the business of the government. A father's maltreatment of a son may result in the personal action of a relative or other individual plus informal social sanctions, but it is unlikely to result in court action. With respect to the Church, the responsibility component tends to fall on the mother; she is the one who both formally and actually is considered to bear the responsibility for her children's Christian upbringing and behavior. As the *Hoja Parroquial* put it, "Her duty to cultivate in her children the Christian virtues is most fundamental and indispensable."

Two factors contribute heavily to the stereotype of authority that the child learns. The first of these is the distance relationship with the father. The child does not observe his father's making of decisions within the walls of the house, for the respect owed the head of the family channels day-to-day authority into the hands of the mother. Respect also demands that the child be away from the father whenever he is on adult male business outside the house; the boy does not gradually learn the role as a result of observing how his father acts vis-à-vis other grown men, for the rules are such that when his father is somewhere outside the house, he is not in the same place. The second factor has to do with the structure of the family itself, its internal splintering, its lack of solidarity within; the father tends to be seen as a free agent rather than as the representative of a nuclear family in reference to the outside world. Solidarity with men in general or with one's leisure companions may have preference.

As a consequence of these factors, the child sees authority as power shorn of responsibility and clothed in the outward symbols of the male role—*machismo* if you will; to be physically strong, careless of consequences and dangers, jealous of one's honor, and able to enforce one's wishes and desires on others. Power is seen as unpredictable, based on personal whims, shaped by *voluntad* (will); the powerful person can bring gifts or mete out punishment, but which he will choose to do cannot be foretold.

The village nuclear family is a particular kind of social world, with a series of definable characteristics. Its patterns of interaction are seen as a network of dyadic relations, its role behavior is strictly defined on the basis of sex and age so that there emerges a set of unique and separate statuses, it is managed and directed in a system of allocation of authority that separates holders of powers and of responsibility, and it is imbedded in a larger household group modeled on the kindred, so that kinship relationship outside the family is ego-centered and not oriented toward any bounded, corporate group.

VIII. THE SOCIAL WORLD OUTSIDE THE HOUSE

IF ONE WERE to consider the class structure of Mexico as a whole, one would find that most of the Tonalá population could be classified in one of the lower groups of the social ladder; a few families might be considered lower middle-class. When Padre Anesagasti wrote his local history toward the end of the last century, he divided the population into two clearly differentiated social groups: *naturales* and *vecinos.* This division presumably rested on racial distinctions. The present population, however, cannot be divided thus; as a matter of fact, given the long-standing custom of barrio endogamy, one wonders whether what the good father was describing was not really a cultural rather than a biological difference. This cultural difference still exists. Although many Tonaltecans are comparatively inarticulate about class differences, they are quite clear on who "we" are and who are "the others." For instance, Policarpio Aceves has for several years contributed money to the festival of the Holy Cross in his barrio—in order to help out his neighbors, he says—but he refuses to take any active part in the proceedings, since he feels that these are customs of "those others" ("los indios" is conveyed silently here). Or when Angel Henríquez, the carpenter—whose income is considerably lower than that of many of his pottery-making neighbors and his education no higher—speaks of local customs, he aligns himself with the *gente de razón* (people with sense), a term usually reserved for those of Spanish rather than Indian heritage. He finds Tonaltecan customs laughably quaint.

The situation is by no means as simple as in Anesagasti's day, when if you were not a vecino, you were a natural. To make the stratification situation more understandable, it is necessary to place the inhabitants in particular pigeonholes derived from the national class structure, and then to consider ranking of individual families.

The traditional class system of the nation was bipartite, consisting of an upper class characterized by the fact that its members did not work with their hands, and of a lower class whose members did. Each class was further subdivided into a plurality of more subtle gradations. The provincial Mexican towns I knew in 1944 had upper classes consisting of a very few members of an upper-upper group, whose position was hereditary, whose style of life splendid, and whose orientation was toward the national or even international scene. Since the source of their wealth had been large landed estates, by that period of post-Revolutionary Mexico either they were beginning to invest in new kinds of enterprises or they were fading off into a Chekhovian twilight. In far greater numbers there were the second group: owners of small private agricultural lands (as contrasted to ejidatarios with use rights in communal lands), men who practiced law and medicine, government officials of some power, and *comerciantes,* ranging from owners of prosperous wholesale businesses to proprietors of grocery stores. The position of these people was based on the fact that they performed no demeaning labor and that they had relatively more wealth than the people below them. However, their style of life was not radically different from the petite bourgeoisie that made up the lower-upper group (salaried workers, clerks, government employees of superior position), or even the upper ranks of the working class. Marriages tended to be made within the two lower sectors of the upper class as a whole. Style of dress, mode of presentation of self, norms, expectations, view of the world, were related to local or at most regional culture.

The overwhelming majority of people stood below the barrier which separated the two classes. Elementary school teachers in government schools, artisans, and skilled workers comprised the group at the top, with unskilled laborers, agricultural workers, ejidatarios, servants, ambulant vendors, and, in some communities, policemen below. At the very bottom were the indigent, the town drunkards, the beggars—the poor deserving of charity, but not respect. Note that although wealth was a necessary adjunct to high status, it did not in and of itself define the class structure. Access to power and the absence of the ritual pollution of manual labor were also taken into account.

Tonalá of old lacked members of several of these categories. It probably had not had a resident member of *flor y nata* (upper-upper, "flower and cream") since Tzihualpilli and her captains lost their hegemony over the region. Within the last century a few families with small to medium landed properties had been resident in the town, but neither lawyers nor physicians had made their home there. The town consisted primarily of a small upper class of independent farmers and storekeepers and a very large lower class of artisans and unskilled workers. Thus the basic bipartite structure was replicated, while the internal membership differed in such a fashion that the townsmen commanded neither economic nor political power in the region or nation.

With an expanding economy the class structure of Mexico has undergone some basic changes. Many observers see an emerging tripartite system with increasing economic and political control in the hands of a new middle class. The analysts' view may indeed reflect the reality of the social scene and the basic dynamics of industrialization, but in the provinces the old scheme lingers on as the participants' model of things. Economic change has meant an increasing emphasis on money (or the acquisition of the symbols of conspicuous consumption) as the source of prestige and increasing political power for the "new middle class," but the continuing importance of the old dichotomy of those who work with their hands and those who don't has preserved the semblance of a two-class system. The man of the provinces assumes that those members of the middle-upper class who have "connections" have usurped the position of the old aristocracy. They are aware that there is a vast gulf in "style of life" between those people and the working class, making their position on top manifest through the possession of new consumer items: automobiles, contemporary houses, overstuffed furniture, the newest of electrical appliances. The symbols shift constantly as yesterday's styles become available to people with less income and prestige, so that even houses become quickly obsolete as builders devise new finishing materials and subdividers develop more fashionable suburbs. Real estate development in Guadalajara bears visible evidence of this using up and throwing away of residences. As employees of the government (who confidently call themselves *burócratas)* acquire better salaries, greater fringe benefits, and more secure positions of power in today's stable regime, they become considered members of the class "who have," thus bearing evidence that there is some social mobility. Although the observer can identify elements of the emerging middle class, the man on the street does not separate out the new entrepreneur, the taker of risks, the long-term investor, the new-style comerciante who is an active agent in a burgeoning economy as a different kind of *rico.*

Present-day Tonalá, like that of traditional times, is composed of a bourgeoisie of storekeepers, owners of small herds of cattle, and landowners. A pharmacist, two priests, a family of wholesale grain dealers, and the owner of the pottery factory complete the inventory. The laboring class far outnumbers them. The largest single group are the potters, but there are agricultural wage laborers and both skilled and unskilled industrial workers who commute to the city as well. Statistics are difficult to amass, for many men support their families by trying their hand at whatever comes their way and by making pottery when agricultural work is slack or when they cannot find other employment. Answers to questionnaires often tended to reflect aspirations rather than cold reality, so that men who lived part of the year by picking over the piles of rubbish that were dumped on agricultural lands as fertilizer and selling the stray piece of iron or cooking pot that came to light saw themselves as comerciantes—at least for the purposes of questionnaires. This attempt to gain respectability was also reflected in the way the federal census questions were answered; before the census was taken the curate urged his congregation to answer all the questions truthfully, for in the previous census Tonalá had come out with an unbelievable number of comerciantes, of eaters of bread rather than tortillas, and wearers of shoes rather than huaraches.

The bourgeoisie of Tonalá expect to maintain their position and their income in the traditional manner through the sale of cash agricultural crops, deals in cattle, and short-term speculation in goods. Their models of ideal behavior are pre-Revolutionary patróns and hacendados, but their decisions are taken according to the precepts: "Buy cheap, sell high," "Watch out for yourself and yours first," "Risk little." The working-class people who concern themselves with social mobility see education as a means of improving and securing their income, but not necessarily as a means of stepping up into the middle class. And regardless of the ideology of egalitarianism taught in school and propounded by orators on public occasions, the mass of Tonaltecans are convinced they are *los pobres.* Even those potters who make contracts with foreign buyers and whose income exceeds that of the city clerk or office worker, when speaking in confidence rather than in reply to formal questioning, refer to themselves as poor, as being Indians, as being ignored and overlooked by the people of power, as having dirty hands—all by the grace of a destiny that made them potters. They tend to look to the middle class for leadership, but the latter are seldom motivated by the principle of *noblesse oblige.*

But the criteria for ranking within Tonalá are complex, and include factors which cannot be attributed to class differences alone. First, there is a town-wide split which gives the farmers a higher rank than the potters. Certain old families of town have automatic respect accorded them.

Such is the case of the N—'s for instance, although they are known as misers, and Don X is considered the Tonalá version of King Farouk, capable of all kinds of dastardies—even incest. The "respect" for the family extends to the point where one of its members, the nearest thing to an outlaw in the region, is allowed to terrorize the poor and helpless without police action.

Tonaltecans are not old Spanish gentlemen who judged a man primarily on the basis of family and occupation; money as an item conferring rank is also important. Standard of living is not always a good guide to a family's wealth, since there are social pressures toward conforming to community patterns of consumption. Another means of gaining or maintaining higher rank is related to the prime means of gaining individual prestige—that of remaining aloof and independent, of not having to ask favors of anyone.

The system of ranking within Tonalá is further reflected in the forms of marriage. Certain families form marriage groups, and marriages made across these lines usually give rise to gossip and criticism. The Martínezes, the Garcías, and the Ramírezes—all owners of land, but none of them wealthy by extra-Tonalá standards—are so interwound that genealogies of these families contain almost no other names. There are instances in which an individual with the patronym García and the same matronym is descended from parents both of whom have identical patronyms and matronyms (according to Spanish usage, both parents and child would be named García García). The other major marriage group consists of certain pottery-making families who tend to make traditional alliances among themselves.

Only a few instances of intermarriage between members of the two groups occur. During my stay in Tonalá one marriage did take place between a young lady of the Martínez family and a young man descended from one of the traditional pottery families. The groom and his family had moved to Mexico City when he was still a young child, and he had received a good education. Although quite young, at the time of the wedding he had been promoted to the position of office manager for the city firm where he worked, and he was earning a respectable income. His family had maintained their ties with Tonalá, and they all regularly came back to their home town on their vacations. It was on one of these visits that the couple fell in love. All of the proper ceremonial steps were taken and the courtship proceeded according to middle-class urban cutsoms. The groom provided the bride with the money for her *donas* (trousseau), and she had a large wardrobe of dresses and suits made. Her new clothes stirred up the usual envy and backbiting comments. ("She should have known better than to get a pleated skirt; with her figure it makes her look like a guitar wrapped in a tablecloth," or, "Maybe it's a good thing she had that dress made in yellow-green, for it hides the bilious look of her complextion.") But the tenor of the remarks over and over again was that she should have saved some of the money, for she would need it to buy food later on. The implicit—and sometimes explicit, depending on the membership of the group—message was that the groom, being a member of a pottery-making family, could not possibly support her financially.

Modes of behavior indicate deference through formality and respect toward certain people. Juan Chávez, a well-known potter, uses a different mode of address in speaking to the Echeverrías, who own the largest grocery store in town, than in speaking to another potter. The greater distance of the relationship would be symbolized by the greater physical distance kept between the participants. If other people pass on the sidewalk while the conversation is in progress, thy would circle around on the street rather than pass between the talkers, for not only the participants but also the observers recognize the nature of the relationship. The vocabulary used in the conversation, and the inflection of the sentences, would be different in a conversation between equals from that between people of different status.

It would be convenient if one could say that every Chávez defers to every Echeverría or Martínez, but such is not the case—even though on the whole the position of the father of a family determines the status of the whole family. This is a ranking, not a completely classificatory system of social stratification. It involves several independent variables; the number of positions on the scale is quite large. Informants tend to rank families, not simply as members of the middle or the lower class, but as either higher, lower, or on the same level as themselves. Marriages and friendships are usually made between families whose ranks are not too disparate. To do otherwise incurs the criticism of being *presumido* (presumptuous). Anyone making friends outside his own immediate group is accused of having ulterior motives (e.g., a man having lower-class friends may be accused of trying to approach the friend's sister—a charge that cannot be made without the brother's taking action; a man seeking to maintain friendships with persons far above him on the ranking ladder might be considered an opportunist or a sycophant).

Second, one's moral and social worth is measured in terms of the individual prestige system. Here again one must differentiate between the set of rules applying to men and those applying to women. In Tonalá as in Alcalá, Spain, and Frontera, Texas, age and education are of importance in the male prestige system (Pitt-Rivers, 1954; Romano, 1960). The attainment of prestige is marked by the use of the title *Don* (roughly equivalent to "sir") by members of the community in addressing and referring to an individual. The simplest requirement for Donship is age, although that characteristic alone is never sufficient. If one has earned the respect of one's neighbors by behaving in a manly and seemly fashion, one becomes an elder, a wise man, a Don. Other men become Dons through other means—by education, by middle- or upper-class status; especially noted potters may even be given the title in recognition of their abilities. Certain kinds of behavior can prevent the earning of the title—drunkards and practical jokers never become Dons even if they are rich, educated, and live to be a hundred years old.

The essential characteristic of the institution of Donship is that it donates position and prestige to the individual on the basis of the central values of the culture as they are expressed in his behavior. The values include independence, manliness, seriousness, formality, education. They are expressed through respectful demeanor, the maintenance of social distance, and the acquisition of wisdom through education and age. Because the essential model of the Don is the patrón, the man who can give favors but need not take them, higher class position adds to the likelihood of acquiring this status, but it is not necessary to it. The poorest man can be addressed as Don. Because the Complete Don (like the Compleat Angler perhaps), as Romano describes him, is a model and an ideal, no single Tonaltecan possesses all his virtues, for no Tonaltecan is able to be completely independent of his fellow townspeople.

The female prestige system has slightly different characteristics. Although chastity is valued almost above all other feminine virtues, and old spinsters have an honorable status of their own, the first requirement for becoming a

Doña is that one must have been married. Secondly, the Doña must be old and preferably widowed. She is usually a woman who has led a life devoted to her family, cloistered from the outside world. She is deeply religious, quiet, humble, self-sacrificing. Fewer women become Doñas than men become Dons.

Third, two other criteria come to be of importance as the distance between Tonalá and Guadalajara becomes less important through increased contact. More than elementary education is now available for many Tonaltecans; being trained for a skilled trade or for a profession are means of raising one's class ranking, but few Tonaltecans take this step.

Since the overt behavior that goes with ranking is the outward sign of the fulfillment or lack of the above criteria, it happens sometimes that the degree of urbanization —particularly in the case of newcomers—in dress and mode of life is taken as evidence of money, respected occupation, and possible education. A Tonaltecan would find it difficult to rise in rank merely by taking on city standards, but even a poor Guadalajaran from the lower end of town is assumed to rank higher than the potters until proved otherwise.

Although ranking tends to be stable, there is some mobility. At present one of the prime means of rising in rank is to acquire more money. In the past, the family which contributed a son to the priesthood also gained status thereby, but now this mode of rising is less important. However, although a technical education is easier to obtain, it does not immediately raise either the individual or his family to a "respect" status. There is somewhat more of a tendency to accord this kind of respect to someone who is believed to have the political power to get things done.

Nevertheless, most of these means of rising socially are only partially effective, for always as a barrier stand the envy and hostility of the townspeople. No successful Tonaltecan is given ungrudging respect or approval. People always accuse him of acting above his station; one hears the constant cliché, "Yo le conocí cuando estaba muriendo de hambre" ("I knew him when he was starving"). In speaking of someone one considers higher in rank, one says, "He thinks he is better than I am," even when the speaker behaves as if he believed it too. The average Tonaltecan knows well the enviousness of his fellows and finds it very difficult to raise his standard of living, even when he can afford to do so, because of the hostility any such move is bound to engender.

In the wider social world, as in the family, there is a split between the locus of power and of responsibility. This kind of differentiation was clear in the day-to-day operations of the municipal government and of decisions made or not made on the community level. In the formal governmental structure the office of municipal president is the principal executive position both for the town and the rural areas of the municipality. The president is the local representative of the executive branch of the federal government as well as the chairman of the basic municipal governing unit, the *ayuntamiento* (municipal council), a body made up of *regidores* or *munícipes* (councillors), elected by popular vote for a term of three years. By a provision of the constitution of the state of Jalisco the ayuntamiento reelects itself annually, thus allowing councillors to expel a member the others consider a weak link or a divisive element in the operations of the municipal government. The president is the First Regidor and has special duties, while the other four are charged with administering the market, municipal parks, the slaughterhouse, street-lighting and street repairs, the cemetery, and garbage collection.

The president's duties are of two kinds: political and administrative. Within the realm of the first of these come such matters as setting up arrangements for elections and holding public speeches on patriotic occasions. Most day-to-day affairs come under the latter set of charges wherein he oversees the maintenance of law and order in the towns, villages, and hamlets of the municipality and sees to the collection of local taxes and the disbursal of funds. He has the power to appoint officials to aid him in his duties—a secretary, police officers, and a city clerk to keep the Civil Register. The treasurer is nominated by the president, but his appointment must have the approval of the state legislature. In Tonalá, since the secretary's duties were not particularly heavy, he also kept the Civil Register and the police records as well as taking care of official correspondence. In very small municipalities the president may choose to perform all or some of these tasks personally. Since these offices are appointive rather than elective, these officials are not subject to the restriction of a three-year term or to the no-reelection rule that applies all over Mexico to elected government posts. In practice secretaries, and rather less frequently treasurers, may serve for long periods of time; in towns like Tonalá, where it is difficult to find someone both competent and willing, the secretary becomes a long-term fixture in the town hall, and he may be the only official who knows how things should be done and how they are done; he is also the continuing link between constantly shifting administrations.

The municipality has specific and limited sources of funds. It collects market fees for the use of space on town streets and sidewalks (or for the rental of stands in a permanent market); it collects fees for the slaughtering of animals in the municipal slaughterhouse; it licenses business establishments; it collects fees for the opening of a grave and charges for a cemetery plot. Annually the state government makes a provisional budget for the municipalities. When the state legislature approves this estimate, it commits the state to make up whatever discrepancy arises between that figure and the actual income to the municipality from its own sources.

The formal structure is to some degree within the tradition of Spanish colonial administration—in the terms used for some offices, in the list of charges to the councillors, in the kinds of matters that come under local taxation, in the very definition of the municipality as an administrative unit. However, among the political reforms undertaken with the writing of both the federal and state constitutions of 1917 was that of breaking the power of local *caciques* (bosses) and of making it impossible for municipalities to become rich at the expense of their citizens. To prevent the ultimate decentralization of governmental processes municipal prerogatives were severely circumscribed and local officials were given little room for initiative or executive action, while the governor was given the right to remove them from office for cause. However, to prevent their being harassed by other officials at the local level, regidores were granted a *fuero* (franchise), giving them freedom from arrest within the state during their term of office except with the explicit action of the state legislature to remove their immunity (by an act of *desafuero*). In towns like Tonalá, with few politically effective contacts with state and federal governments, with exceedingly small treasuries at their disposal, officials are at best only able to maintain elementary services and cannot undertake programs of urban renewal and beautification.

Some presidents have been able to exercise power either

through serendipity, the indifference of officials in Guadalajara, or their own personal attributes, while others were viewed as time-servers and tools of the real power-holders in the formal structure. One of the latter type was given the significant and sarcastic nickname of La Peligrosa (The Dangerous Woman), for in the Tonalá social universe to be powerful is to be male. The effective political leader is the independent macho who can command that things be done. It is within his power to bestow favors, and it is also within his power to withhold them. Since being a powerful leader requires at least the tacit recognition of his role as a strong man, a leader who does not assume some of the outward aspects of the macho role can get nothing done.

The 1958 municipal election was a good illustration of this point. While the entire town is composed of 36 blocks, early in the campaign there were 24 candidates for presidente municipal, each supported by a small band of followers tied to him by various particularistic bonds: kinsmen, compadres, patróns, clients, neighbors.

Mexican politics have long been dominated by a single party (Partido Revolucionario Mexicano, PRM, and its successor, Partido Revolucionario Institucional, PRI), although other parties have arisen and, in some cases, managed to survive. The strongest of the latter is PAN (Partido de Acción Nacional), comprised of elements more conservative than those of PRI. It has had considerable appeal generally in Jalisco and has several enthusiastic supporters in Tonalá. However, it has concentrated on the national and state levels of politics, and has not nominated candidates for local offices. Tonaltecan *panistas* must content themselves with talk and painting slogans on walls. Other opposition parties have also failed to run candidates for municipal posts. Consequently, the official party nomination is tantamount to election. It was important then for the prospective candidates to offer evidence of town support to party officials in order to obtain the PRI nomination. The situation was stalemated until a candidate for president and one for treasurer joined forces. Their slate was the only one which looked as if it had any sizable grass-roots support, both men had the approval of the party hierarchy, and they were nominated and elected. Since then, however, the townspeople as a whole have disclaimed any commitment to their municipal government. The president and treasurer cannot even rely on the wholehearted support of their personal followers, and since the mayor has no popular mandate, neither his suggestions nor direct commands are followed.

Admiring stories are told about certain politicians who come to personify the Good Political Leader. In 1960 the political hero was the late governor of Jalisco, González Gallo, who was responsible for many of the urban improvements in Guadalajara. The content of all tales is the same: The Governor decided one day he wanted a new park in a particular block. The owners of the property objected, for they did not want to give up their homes and businesses. They took the matter to court, and the judge issued an injunction to prevent the Governor from having the buildings torn down. After a while, González Gallo became angry at the delay and decided to act. Early one morning he went to the spot with soldiers (or bulldozers, depending on which version of the folktale is being told) and told them to tear the buildings down. After his orders had been carried out, many of the property-owners died from the effects of the fits of anger which had come over them.

The fact that the Governor allegedly was able to get his way without going through legal processes is considered a sign that he was strong and manly.

The same picture of the nature of political leadership emerges from one informant's account of why the Tonaltecan water project was a failure:

"The trouble is that the officials here do not know how to go about doing something like this. Now they say that we have to request to have pipes put in and pay for it. That is not the way those things are done. I know from when I was up in Mexicali that when a real urbanization project is undertaken, they just go ahead and make the installations first and then make the people pay for it. They don't come around and ask you whether you want water or sewers, they just put them in. But the way it is being done here, we will never get anywhere."

This conversation continued with a contradiction which suggests that by whatever means a project is put through, neither are the people responsible to the leaders nor is the leader responsible to the people:

"When they first began installing the water system, they put in the main pipe and then began putting the pipes into some houses. Then they wanted to start charging the common people. We told them. "You can't do that. We didn't ask for the water, and we don't want it." They went ahead and piped water in from a dam about five kilometers away, and then they told us the main pipe alone cost twenty thousand pesos. It couldn't really have cost that much, especially because the pipe is just asbestos."

This mutually reinforcing contradiction is related to the informant's view that the local officials do not have enough power to force through their wishes. They cannot marshal soldiers and bulldozers and leave opponents dying of fury.

The expectations of followers as to the nature of leadership affects the way leaders must behave. Even the mild-mannered priest of Tonalá was caught in this situation at the time the building of the existing water system of Tonalá was being discussed. In order for the community to obtain federal aid to help finance the project, it was necessary to prove to the federal agency concerned that the town was willing to support the project and to undertake some of the financial responsibility for its installation and maintenance. The Tonaltecans as a whole were reluctant. The more conservative elements among the population felt that piping in water was an unnecessary modern frill, for the old system of hauling water jugs by burros was satisfactory.

Discussions had gone on for some time to no avail, and the future of the project was in jeopardy. The priest was convinced that a water system was urgently needed and determined to help gain public support. During Easter Week when all the community was attending a series of religious retreats through which a reinvigoration of Christian faith and way of life was to be attained, the priest decided to take action. At the close of the last session with the adult men, he ordered the doors of the church to be locked and announced that no one was to leave until the matter of the water project had been settled. A consensus was not easily reached. The debate went on for some time with many men still opposed, although the moral leadership of the priest was convincing to the others. Finally approval was obtained, but what was never clearly understood by the Tonaltecans was that this was to be as much their water project as the federal government's, and that they had both administrative and financial obligations toward it. The townspeople thought that they were asked for their permission to be donated a water system; the federal government officials thought they were helping the initiation of a cooperative community project. Consequently, at present the financial status of the Tonalá water agency is in a serious way. Townspeople refuse to pay their share of the maintenance costs, for they view these expenses as extortion. After all, they had been given a water system by President Alemán.

During the year I spent in Tonalá, a new water project seemed necessary, for the old one proved spectacularly insufficient. The priest wishes this time to serve only in an advisory capacity, for he is convinced his previous methods were questionable, and he does not wish to do the same thing again. The entire proceedings leading to the setting up of the old system have been reinterpreted by the townspeople to make the actual events conform even more closely with the existing stereotype of the nature of political affairs. One informant's account is as follows:

"The water project was begun during Don Juan's term in office and completed during his compadre's time. You can imagine how much influence Don Juan has—President Alemán himself came to the inauguration. It was either through Don Juan or the Señor Cura [the priest] who is a doctor or lawyer or both and who has lots of influence in the government."

The possibility of having a new water system installed was under constant discussion. Several attempts were made to initiate a new project, with the support of the presidente municipal, the federal deputy, the priest, and the members of the elected Water Committee in charge of the present system. There was no active opposition, but there was little grass-roots support either. On several occasions plans were made for a delegation to obtain the help of state and federal officials, but no attempts were made to seek community-level support. Finally, the more interested citizens decided to appeal directly to the governor. The priest, the chairman of the Water Committee, and a few of the more prominent citizens from around the plaza convinced the president to appoint a committee. He named several members of the Water Committee, a personal representative of the federal deputy, and himself to the delegation. No survey as to the nature of the problem or the possibility of its solution had been prepared (although my husband had suggested that it might be better to have a detailed program to present for consideration).

The matter was done in typical provincial fashion: the delegation was gathered together at dawn; it proceeded to the home of the federal deputy in Guadalajara to get official blessing, and then finally arrived in the anterooms of the governor with the hope of making the petition. Since no appointment had been arranged, the villagers had a long wait, but were finally interviewed by the governor's secretary. When asked what it was they wished, the spokesman answered bluntly, "The town of Tonalá wants water."

The secretary asked the logical questions: "How much water? From what source? How much will the project cost? What financial support does the town offer?" As there were no answers, the secretary told them to go back to Tonalá, to survey the situation, and then to return for an appointment with the governor. Their request would be given every consideration.

The committee followed only the first of his suggestions. Once the members were back home, they complained that the governor did not like Tonalá, that he offered them no help. Within the following five months that I was there, no further action was taken.

The sequence of expectations—petition and gift with no further responsibilities—was also exemplified in another incident which occurred that year. Just previous to my taking up residence in Tonalá, a playground had been built and equipped through the initiation of the federal deputy. Local funds were raised at a town bazaar, supported also by a group of prominent women from Guadalajara (who undertook the activity in the name of charity) and some of the Tonaltecans. Sufficient money was collected from all sources to buy inexpensive playground equipment and to whitewash a room in the town hall to serve as a public library. A few bookshelves, a table, and benches were also supplied. The school personnel cooperated by painting murals on the blank walls facing the playground and planting a few small pine trees. The new public facilities were inaugurated on Independence Day with a parade, ceremonies, and all public dignitaries present.

Shortly thereafter the usual difficulties arose. No one wished to be responsible for the maintenance of the facilities. The schoolteachers and the school director felt that they had been slighted in the ceremonies and the municipal officials had taken more than their share of credit. When the president suggested that a playground and a library properly fell within the administrative jurisdiction of the school, they rebelled and refused to have anything further to do with either. The president maintained that he had neither personnel for keeping the playground clean nor funds for equipping the library. Since the school director refused to cooperate, he locked the playground the day after the inauguration. From then on, for a whole year, it remained locked while the children climbed over and burrowed under the fence. In a year's time there was nothing left of the playground, while no library was ever set up at all.

The response of both individuals and the community as a whole to cooperative efforts indicates that no project can be maintained in the face of the existing attitudes toward responsibility. As long as Tonaltecans depend upon the *bondad y gentileza* (kindness and nobility) of outsiders and of powerful politicians, they will not develop the prerequisites for corporate action: personal commitment to the goals of the group, a sense of solidarity with and responsibility to one's fellow members, and a concept of representative leadership.

Territoriality does, however, provide a basis for defining membership in a group (Lewis, 1960: p. 51). Traditionally the most important social division in Tonalá has been the cuartel system. It provided both a means of dividing the town into smaller social units and a basis for the formation of solidary groups. Until the late 1940's the cuartel system provided a means for the expression of hostility. The young men of a cuartel would occasionally make forays or raids into the cuarteles, sometimes only making un escándalo. The all-Tonalá festival honoring St. James, the town's patron saint, annually was enlivened or marred, depending on the point of view, by inter-cuartel fights after the dance reenacting the Spanish Conquest. Palm Sunday was also punctuated by fighting as the cuartel contingents carried their plaited palm leaves to the church. On Sundays when the plaza was crowded with people, trouble would break out, and sometimes a small shooting war would ensue. People of the region looked on Tonalá as an unsafe and violent town, and state and federal officials made several attempts at "de-pistolizing" the townspeople.

When the present priest appeared on the scene, he was scandalized at the violent behavior of his parishioners. Since exhortations and sermons did nothing to better the situation, he tried a new strategy. He organized a series of religious associations based, not on cuartel unity as the old ones had been, but on age and sex. Unmarried and married men and women became members of separate sections of Acción Católica. He tried to encourage those religious associations which were not organized on barrio lines, and he eliminated the traditional dances from the festival of St. James. His principal concern was the breaking up of cuartel solidarity by removing religious validation from cuartel organization.

To a great extent he succeeded. Tonalá is pacific. People from Guadalajara say the Indians have finally been subjugated and civilized, while the Tonalá priest characterized his parishioners as "humildes, amables, y mansos" (humble, amiable, and tame).

The cuartel structure is not completely destroyed, however. It retains considerable symbolic and ritual significance. Its continuing importance is most readily apparent in the local specialization in pottery production and in the physical arrangement of the pottery market (see chap. ix). Certain religious associations are still connected with specific barrios; the association dedicated to St. Joseph, for instance, is considered to belong to Cuartel 4. The organization of the ceremonies on the day of San Isidro follows cuartel lines. Palm Sunday rituals are performed on a cuartel basis. On the previous Saturday in each cuartel men gather in the home of *el grande* (the big man) of the Palm Sunday *hermandad* (brotherhood). The night is spent in plaiting palm leaves into intricate shapes and in drinking and conviviality. The traditional procession the next morning has been eliminated at the suggestion of the priest, for it used to be the occasion for inter-cuartel hostilities. However, he was unable to eliminate the cuartel solidarity rite of the night before. For one year only the villagers moved into the church atrium for the plaiting, the priest having agreed that they would be served a drink apiece in order to follow the traditional pattern. But a festival with only one drink was *muy desabrida* (without savor) according to the local men, and they returned to holding separate cuartel drinking parties.

The cuartel organization is symbolized and validated by rituals other than religious ones. Soccer, a late addition to Tonalá culture, has become entrenched, probably since it has become an instrument for the expression of the divisions in the social structure. The soccer teams are relevant both to the maintenance of the cuartel system and to the tendencies toward fusing sections of the cuarteles into age-graded organizations.

Five of the teams represent individual barrios and draw almost all their membership from a single cuartel (two groups come from Cuartel 1; all others are represented by a single team). Three of the teams represent the fusion tendency. In the first place, the Santiago team sponsored by Acción Católica reflects another side of the priest's effort to create some kind of civic unity by supporting all-Tonalá organizations. The pottery factory sponsors a team among its workers, thus creating a secular symbol of town unity as contrasted with the Santiago team (which is usually referred to as "the priest's team"). The third "barrio-fusion" team represents another geographical and social split in Tonalá. It draws its members from all four barrios, but is considered to represent *los del centro* (the people from the center of town). The people around the plaza are generally considered to belong to a higher social class than those from *las orillas* (the edges). They comprise Tonalá's social register—storekeepers, owners of large plots of farm land, and cattle owners.

The cuartel structure is still of importance in the selection of a spouse. There are no overt obligatory rules as to endogamy nowadays, but social interaction still tends to take place predominantly along barrio lines. Tonaltecans interpret barrio endogamy as "marrying one's childhood sweetheart." Twenty years ago one did not marry out because people from other barrios were "the enemy"; now one does not marry out because they are strangers.

To the villagers the barrios are still real social entities. Since most adults can remember back to the time that inter-barrio aggression was not channeled into team sports, the symbolic aspect of the lines of organization of athletic teams and of religious associations and festivals is very clear to them. They also feel that the cuartel to which they belong gives them part of their social identity. In a town of six thousand people it is almost impossible to recognize everyone on the basis of face-to-face knowledge, but people can bc identified by the barrio affiliation. Outside of his immediate acquaintanceship a Tonaltecan knows a fellow villager as "one of the farmers from Cuartel 3," "one of the Colorados of Cuartel 4," "the baker in Cuartel 2," "the lame man from the Third Cuartel," or "the witch of Cuartel 1."

Less important than the barrio division is that which separates the village into eastern and western halves. For the thirty years from 1910 to 1940 this division was represented symbolically by two churches: the parish church in the east and Sacred Heart in the west. In the interests of town solidarity the priest decided that the town should have one church only, and nowadays he refuses to say Mass in the western half except twice a year. The building itself is maintained by an association of interested women from the western half who sweep and dust and see to it that someone says the Rosary in the chapel every evening. During June, the month of the Sacred Heart of Jesus, this group decorates the church and pays for the Mass to be celebrated. Once a year, however, this church becomes the center for the activity of half the town. There still exists, among the men of the first and second cuarteles, an association which organizes and supports a celebration for the Christ Child held in the Church of the Sacred Heart on Christmas Day. Aside from paying for a special Mass, the association provides fireworks and a *castillo* (pyrotechnic set piece), making sure that the pyrotechnic display equals that at the parish church for the Virgin of Guadalupe earlier in December. The year I was in the village this celebration was marked by a singular event—on Christmas morning the image of the Christ Child was stolen. The association provided another figure by the time of the evening Rosary, but the original image was not found. The culprits were assumed to be people from the eastern half of town by some westerners, city riffraff by those loyal to the town as a whole, or atheistic *agraristas* (farmers who work ejido lands) by militant conservatives.

The final important social division is that of the nine districts connected with the Holy Cross celebration. These nine areas may represent the vestiges of the original pre-Conquest barrio system; the names of the Fourth Cuartel are suggestive of Nahuatl: *Kas teo chepe* and *Kas teo Galván* (the latter word being a common last name in Tonalá, clearly of Spanish origin). Magdalena Covarrubias pointed out that all the crosses are connected with a water hole within the confines of the village. It is interesting, but not unexpected, that water sources are important enough in Tonalá life to make them the center of a series of big annual festivities. Despite the fact that this festival celebrates a day no longer officially a feast day in the Catholic calendar, and despite continuous clerical opposition to their "folk customs" since the turn of the century, Tonaltecans celebrate the Holy Cross in their traditional way. Clerics in the state generally are increasingly reluctant to put up with what they view as indigenous and pagan customs. The present curate's dissatisfaction with this celebration also stems from his observation that it perpetuates the barrio and intra-barrio divisions of a town that, in his words, lacks "collective solidarity." The Tonalá priest has announced that for no price will he celebrate Mass at the site of the chapels built for this festival.

The festival is under the responsibility of an hermandad for each district. The precise details of membership and obligations vary somewhat from one district to another, but the traditional basis of organization is similar. The following description of the organization of the White Cross of the Second Cuartel follows the typical pattern of these societies, although there is some variation. The initial planning is done by twelve *cargadores* who elect four *comisiones* from among their membership. The latter then speak to their friends and neighbors in the district to obtain thirty-six volunteers, who become *oficiales*. Preliminary organizational meetings are called by setting off fireworks. Cargadores, comisiones, and oficiales convene. The cargadores must provide the oficiales with chocolate and sweet bread for the evening's refreshment. It may take several meetings to decide the details connected with the festival—kind of music, amount of fireworks, how to budget the available finances.

This festival runs as a novena but the celebrations are usually staggered somewhat so that the climax of the fiesta—the ninth day—varies from district to district, but always falls somewhere during the week of May third. The dates are arranged by the comisiones (or in some districts a *mayordomo*) in conjunction with the priest. The festival organizers, with the help of their families, construct a chapel of poles and cloths to house the cross of the district. (Two crosses are in permanent chapels.) A steplike altar is made of boards resting on benches and covered with a sheet and decorated with flowers arranged in rows of vases on the altar before the cross. Each group tries to outdo the others; arrangements are elaborate and often artistically pleasing—all white lilies, white gladioli and pink hydrangeas, or two-toned roses.

Each night of the novena the people of the district are called to Rosary by fireworks (also provided by the cargadores). Oficiales (or members of their family sent as representatives) are served *agua fresca* (fruit punch) provided by the cargadores. Outside the chapel the neighborhood women set up tables to sell tacos, tostadas, and pozole, but this aspect of the festival is separate from the formal organization. Anyone can try to sell anything he wishes. Nevertheless, part of the gaiety of the festival is directly connected with the impression of abundance and feasting. Groups of cargadores and oficiales are expected to keep awake each night alternately praying and singing, but on the evening before the last day they all convene. At that time each cargador turns over his charge to a successor from among the oficiales, while fireworks are set off to mark the completion of each transfer of charge. The former cargador then gives his successor a bottle of tequila, and the bottles circulate around. To make the transactions reciprocal, as all Tonaltecan transactions are, the oficiales provide each cargador with a mug of atole blanco and a French roll.

The final day is marked by a great assemblage of fireworks during calls to the dawn Mass and a band to play mañanitas from the chapel to the church. The cross, if it is a portable one, is carried in the procession. During the day more fireworks signal various events—the arrival of the *danzantes*. Most Tonaltecans agree that the quality of the folk dance performance has deteriorated. In the past, for instance, one district specialized in a Dance of the Conquest with some parts spoken and acted. Nowadays the *danza* tends to be a general rhythmic stamping accompanied by tin rattles of a self-consciously "Indian" or "Aztec" variety. A fiddle and the long horizontal slit drum (*petenahuaxtle* in Tonalá; *teponatzli* in San Atzingo, see Bushnell) provides the music for the dance. The dancers—men, boys and girls—represent "Indians" but there is also a good-sized group of "grotesques" called *negros* in Tonalá—boys and young men dressed in old clothes and wearing animal or ugly human masks and carrying a stick or rope whip. They are the comedians or clowns of the occasion.

Alternating with the danzas, the hired bands play the usual Sunday evening repertoire—overtures, nineteenth-century Mexican songs, Viennese waltzes. In the past the culmination of the festival was an *encuentro de músicos* (battle of musicians) held in the main plaza. All the bands from the nine districts convened in the plaza after the last castillo. Each band would occupy a separate spot, and there would follow an endurance contest to see which band had *más resistencia* (more resistance). This grand finale came to an end after an evening in which a hired band from the town of Jocotepec was beaten by a local band. Insults and fighting followed. Since that time the civil authorities have refused to give permission for more encuentros de músicos. The end of the celebrating comes now when the castillos are set off before midnight, as in a final blaze of glory there is consumed the last installment of the pounds of powder used to bring praise to the Holy Cross.

It is important to recognize that these groups are organized and maintained on a highly traditional basis and for the express purpose of the celebration of the collective symbol of a neighborhood district in opposition to the others of the community. The traditional aspect was made clear in the events which occurred in the Second Cuartel the year previous to my fieldwork. The cargadores of the White Cross decided to modernize the festival and to avoid having to depend on raising money from oficiales. It would be less trouble and more civilized to raise the money by each contributing one hundred pesos, they felt, and they could thereby also eliminate some of the traditional frills such as serving chocolate and bread. They soon ran into trouble. Several cargadores failed to fulfill their pledge. One cargador had gone to the United States as a farm laborer, and wrote, resigning from his post since he would not be present at the festival. Two others found they had unexpected expenses and could not raise the money. Consequently the remaining cargadores had to plan an economy fiesta.

The second problem was that since there were no longer 36 oficiales to attend the Rosary, the evening crowd was smaller and the affair seemed less important. The people of the barrio commented that it was almost as if they had no festival at all and they felt shamed before the rest of the town. Since there were no oficiales present, the cargadores took to absenting themselves from the Rosary and the wake also (a good demonstration that cooperation in Tonalá is seen as balanced opposition).

But most important of all, once the traditional organization was abandoned, there was no means of recruiting leaders for the festival of the next year. In order to hold a fiesta the following year in the district the same cargadores had to volunteer for a second term. Most of them agreed albeit reluctantly, for they felt the honor of the neighborhood required a festival. It seems clear that maintenance of the group organization depends upon the performance of the traditional ritual.

In addition, the group is considered to have functions only in reference to the performance of ritual. No villager sees the possibility of using the existing traditional organizations for other purposes. They are not the nuclei around which to form mutual loan funds, marketing cooperatives, or civic organizations. If a brotherhood has particularly energetic members, they concentrate their activities on elaborating already existing patterns: more fireworks, more flowers, better music. Occasionally newly elected cargadores are eager to undertake some project. It usually takes the form of obtaining money from volunteers for a new cross, a permanent chapel, or the renovation of an existing one. One economically significant result of the round of religious festivals is that some of the small capital acquired by members of the societies is used for ceremonial rather than reinvestment.

The last type of corporate group which exists in Tonalá is also oriented primarily toward ritual and religious expression. These are the religious associations which meet in the church. The list is rather lengthy, but gives some idea of the devout religious flavor of the town: Acción Católica in its four sections (young men, young ladies, married women, adult men), the Brotherhood of our Lady of Refuge, the Associations of the Perpetual Vigil, the Association of the Apostolic Society of Prayer (Sacred Heart of Jesus), the Daughters of the Immaculate Mary, the Gardeners of the Host, the Association of the Holy Angels, the Mexican Nocturnal Adoration, Brotherhood of Our Lady of Guadalupe, the Association of St. Joseph.

Most of the associations include members of both sexes, but the groups meet as separate sections, each having its own set of officers. The leadership of groups rests in the hands of the priest who meets with them. (Tonalá has a curate in charge of the parish and an additional priest to help). In these associations the priest is the final arbiter in all decisions. Indeed, in his absence it is felt that nothing can be done, and the meeting may become an informal gossip session or an evening of individual prayers. The associations are oriented primarily toward the performance of religious duties; this is true even in cases where the national bodies of these associations stress other goals as well (as does Acción Católica). Thus villagers list the following religious obligations as the duty of members of Catholic Action: to confess and take communion before all important religious holidays, to take part in all religious processions, to display the association banner on certain Sundays of the month, to take turns to *velar el Santíssimo* (stand vigil over the Host) during the course of the year. Aside from attending weekly meetings and organizing a kermis occasionally to raise money for the flowers and candles needed for ritual obligations, these are the functions of the sections of Catholic Action. The response is typical of Tonalá in that it lists the duties of individuals, but does not lay any stress on corporate action. The young ladies of Acción Católica planned a picnic once, but then only because the chapter had received an admonishing letter from the regional office in Guadalajara. In the city, Acción Católica officials see the organization as a means of providing healthy and approved recreation under supervision. In the village the organization is seen as a means of convening a group of individuals for Christian instruction and ritual.

Part of the charm of association membership lies in the possession of banners and regalia. All associations have scapularies in colors symbolizing the saint they are dedicated to and banners to be carried in processions. Some also specify special clothing on important occasions: black trousers and white shirts for the young men of Acción

Católica, white blouses and pleated skirts for the girls of Acción Católica, black dresses and head scarves for the women of the Daughters of Mary.

On one occasion a religious association did take action in a civic matter. For almost a month Tonalá had been without street lights, for the municipal electric bill had not been paid to the city utility company, during which time there had been a great deal of complaining, but no direct action. When action did come, it came from unexpected quarters. The Guadalajara newspapers were informed by agents unknown, but guessed to be the young men of Acción Católica, that Tonalá was without lights, and the Sunday serenata would be held by torchlight. The instigators also collected a small sum of money at the Saturday soccer game.

On Sunday evening large bonfires were made in the streets coming into the plaza. Torches were set up to light the kiosk. The evening was a gala affair as the participants played their roles *con brío:* the young men offered their girl friends lighted candles rather than the customary flowers, the girls pretended they could not recognize their suitors in the dim light and had to hold a lighted candle in front of their faces in order to recognize friend from foe. Everyone was exceptionally lighthearted at a masquerade in which only the darkness provided the disguises.

The following afternoon an article appeared in the Guadalajara paper, taking the Tonalá municipal president to task. The newspaper article came to the attention of the federal deputy for the district, and when he insisted on looking at the town accounts, a discrepancy of thirteen thousand pesos was discovered. The treasurer was allowed to resign with the understanding that he would reimburse the town, and a new treasurer was appointed, a doctor residing in the city but holding weekly consultations in the town. The lights were turned on again after the power company was assured payment.

One can take this instance as the exception that proves the rule in Tonalá corporate action. Three things are important to note: (1) the action taken was dramatic and easily organized, (2) it was designed to push outsiders into making final decisions and taking responsible action, and (3) it required performance at only one time, not the constant decision and activity involved in the maintenance of a project.

In Tonalá, as contrasted with some villages in Mexico, a series of corporate bodies can be identified with membership defined either on the basis of locality or of age. If one or the other criterion were adhered to, it is possible that the community could be composed of exclusive corporate groups, each with its own leadership and understood functions; these in turn could become instruments for dealing with some of the situations in which a traditional village must adapt to an industrial nation. However, in Tonalá a series of other matters interfere and prevent the development of permanent factions, pressure groups, or cooperatives:

(1) Existing corporate groups serve only ritual functions. At least until now there has been little recognition by the villagers of their serving as a basis for other kinds of activities.

(2) The organization of one kind of group is highly traditional and integrated into the performance of ritual. In this group the decisions of leaders are restricted to *administrative* acts: what day the festival is to be held, how many rockets are to be employed. Leaders cannot make decisions from a wide set of alternatives or initiate new kinds of action. Attempts to do so threaten the continuance of the group.

(3) Groups which meet in the church are directed by outsiders—for in the town the priests represent the city and the national culture. Again the leaders within the group are not empowered to make executive decisions.

(4) Activities undertaken by such groups are single performances: a bazaar, the celebration in honor of a saint, the ritualized expression of opposition to another group. Action undertaken could be characterized as an act of praise or a protest rather than as a program. It is assumed that "something would be done" by outsiders once the protest has been made. This is the kind of politically oriented action that Hobsbawm (1961) calls prepolitical and characteristic of the millenarian movements of South European peasants.

It seems clear that neither social planners nor Tonaltecans can utilize existing corporate groups in order to do some of the things necessary for "progress," however it be defined. Tonaltecan potters do not try to use their religious brotherhoods as pottery-marketing cooperatives. City or local politicians do not find the existing groups suitable nuclei for building civic improvement agencies. The structure with its weakly defined power roles is unsuitable for the initiation of new action. It is even less suitable for maintaining any long-term project. The additional factor which prevents the emergence of the existing voluntary associations as agencies of action and change lies in the ideology of the Mexican Revolution, and the Tonaltecan's view of their relationship to the Church and the state. The clerical revolution of the 1920's, the Cristero revolt, marked the complete break between the revolutionary anticlerical government and the Church. In Tonalá there was little doubt where one's loyalties lay. There were a few villagers who felt that the government represented the side of the potter and the peasant, but most of them allied themselves with the Cristero forces against "atheistic, socialist politicians." This view of the government has hardly been modified at all in the last thirty years. Its agents are assumed to be un-Christian, grafting opportunists. Obviously they cannot expect the cooperation of the religious associations of the village.

Aside from the associations organized for religious purposes there are no corporate groups in the village. There are no permanent factions aside from the small, ineffective ejido group (see chap. ix); there are no patterns of personal allegiances clustering to form informal but bounded social circles. Factions are *ad hoc,* formed for a given situation, and they disintegrate quickly. Even kinship ties, if outside the household unit, do not produce stable, bounded corporate groups.

When a villager speaks of parientes (relatives) outside his nuclear family and outside the household unit, he is referring to a personal kindred. Kinship is reckoned bilaterally and outward from ego. But the kindred is not defined on the basis of fixed boundaries, as in some societies where "my relatives" refers to descendants of common great-grandparents, or to all relatives within a set number of connecting links. The kindred comprises all those people who are consanguineally related to ego and with whom he expects to have mutually reciprocal obligations. Other factors may intervene to exclude people one would normally expect to recognize as kinsmen. Geographical distance in particular affects whether consanguineal relatives are perceived as members of one's kindred. A mother's brother's son who lives in another cuartel may be loosely referred to as "somehow related to me," but may never be called on for favors or never invited to life-cycle events because a regular pattern of social interaction was not established. A father's brother who lives in another state may lose all ties with his Tonalá nephews and nieces unless the relationship is validated through favors performed or received.

This fact points up something important about Tonalá social structure. Although social relationships are formed primarily on particularistic grounds, outside the nuclear family and the household, the basis for their establishment is not kinship. Rather the social ties are made on the basis of social contract (Foster, 1961) and of territoriality.

The social contract at its most formal level is that between two compadres (co-godparents). The general phenomenon of *compadrazgo* (co-godparenthood) is well known in the literature on Mexico (e.g., Foster, 1953a, and Mintz and Wolf, 1950). It results from the practice of using sponsors at various life-cycle rites. The important social tie established is that between the godparents and the real parents, a tie validated through the sponsorship in the sacred ritual and, ideally speaking, continued through a lifetime. Theoretically, parents can choose as sponsor for their children and prospective compadres either relatives or friends, social equals or superiors, but the choice, while seemingly on an individual basis, is not completely random.

In Tonalá there are regular sponsors (padrinos) for the following occasions: baptism, confirmation, first communion, and weddings. In addition there may be padrinos for a housewarming, for the image of the Christ Child in the Christmas crèche, or for mock weddings at church bazaars. Compadrazgo formed on the basis of these latter occasions is not a serious matter, but is rather seen as a lighthearted joke, and no permanent obligations arise through such sponsorship. Baptismal padrinos are considered the most important kind of godparents and baptismal compadres the most important ritual kinsmen. They are expected to pay for the clothes the child wears to the baptism. Sometimes padrinos also give the child a keepsake—a ring, a gold chain, or a rosary—but such a gift is not obligatory. The contract between compadres is not completely sealed until the child's parents have given a party in honor of the padrinos. In one case, where the parents were unable to finance such a fiesta, the godparents refused to address them as compadres thereafter, although they felt they still had the padrinos' usual responsibility toward the child. Padrinos are expected to see to it that their godchildren receive a Christian education and attend *doctrina* (catechism school) regularly, but in practice many padrinos neglect this duty. If the child dies, the padrinos provide the casket, some of the flowers and, if it is a girl child, a little crown. In one instance, when a child died whose padrinos had had a falling out with the parents, the godparents made no move toward ordering a coffin. The parents waited a whole day, but not hearing from their compadres, the father sought out the padrino and shouted at him, "¿Se lo entierro o se lo como?" ("Shall I bury him or eat him?")

The ritual kinsman has other obligations than those toward the child. Those people who address each other as compadre have entered a relationship with reciprocal obligations. They invite each other to the fiestas held in their homes to celebrate marriages or saints' days. They can rely on their compadres' support at times of crisis. If they need to borrow work animals or money, the first person to ask is a compadre. If they need extra hands at harvest time or are themselves unable to work because of illness, they can call on a compadre. Relations between compadres are expected to be respectful, friendly (although not necessarily intimate) and somewhat formal. Nevertheless, actual unfriendly relations are not unusual. Cross-sex compadre relationships are hedged in by the restrictions usual to cross-sex relations of any kind and are characterized by formal courtesy, respect, and distance. *Comadres'* (co-godmothers) relationships are traditional or intimate in a legendary way. The common expression for gossiping is *comadrear,* but as with many legends, it is only partly true. There are comadres who are very friendly and who visit each other frequently, but this is because they were friends and visited frequently before they were comadres; that is, the intimacy springs from other causes than their co-godparenthood. As a matter of fact, *comadreando* is of such low repute that many lean over backward to avoid the allegation, and restrict their interaction with their comadre to formal occasions. A Tonalá woman gains personal prestige by sticking to the house and to business as much as possible.

Baptismal godparents are usually chosen from among social equals; indeed the ideal pattern as stated by the villagers is to choose relatives. The sponsors for first communion and confirmation, however, are often chosen from persons considered of higher rank or greater wealth. In such cases the compadres become patron and client. The owner of the pottery factory is usually padrino for the sons of all his employees for first communion, providing candles and flowers for the ceremony, which is performed annually when the bishop comes for a visit. There is established then a relationship which is seen as mutually beneficial; Don Pascual can count on the personal loyalty of his employees, and they can turn to him for loans or patronage.

The proliferation of compadrazgo relationships does not go on endlessly. There is a marked preference for restricting the number of people with whom one establishes the relationship and intensifying already existing ones. According to the ideal pattern, one chooses compadres from among one's immediate relatives (although an analysis of the church register revealed this practice was not followed as often as the villagers thought—82 cases in which compadres were unrelated, 23 of paternally related compadres and 25 maternally). One often prefers to choose the same godparents for the first three children. The padrino feels it is his right to be godfather for three children in the family. As one informant said, "After being padrino for one child, he has the right to expect two more in order to make the cross" ("tiene el derecho que le entreguen dos más para hacer la cruz"). Unless the baptismal godparents are the maternal grandparents, it is preferred that they serve as sponsors at their godchild's wedding also.

When one has become the padrino for three children in the family, the baptismal party is considered especially important. The compadres embrace formally and say, "Now we are compadres three ways." The three-times-compadre bond is supposed to indicate a particular social and spiritual closeness. Clearly in Tonalá the compadre system is characterized by intensification of already existing bonds rather than the extension and ramification into new ones.

The compadrazgo system joins pairs of individuals into networks of social relations. Friendship, although not formally validated by ritual, follows the same pattern (Foster, 1961). As is common everywhere, friendship is established on the basis of common experiences, sympathetic personalities, and proximity. The rights and duties involved are, however, culturally determined and fit into the pattern of expectations of the compadrazgo system. One exchanges goods and services in a system where balance is never actually struck, but wherein each party expects to come out evenly in the long run. The system keeps running because to give means prestige and to receive puts one temporarily in debt. This mutual and reciprocal exchange of gifts and favors is the stereotype for the Tonaltecans' model of social interaction.

Social action is seldom seen as motivated by general principles or related to internalized values. Josefa provided the clearest illustration of this. We had been discussing bride-stealing, and I told her of an incident that had occurred in another town. A resentful former suitor had snatched a girl and carried her off against her will. Several people saw her being abducted, and although they noted that she was fighting back, no one went to help her. The person who had told me the story had later asked some of the bystanders why they had not stepped in. Someone responded that the girl had not asked them to interfere. She had screamed, but she had not said, "Help me," so they had concluded it was none of their business. Josefa clucked appropriately over the story and then added her own comment, "Was there no one there who was a friend of hers? Or even if not, you would think that someone would remember that if they did someone else a favor that some day the favor would be returned." The statement sounds like a rewording of the Golden Rule, but considering the context, it would mean that one does not owe a duty to the community as a whole to maintain certain standards of law and order, but that one's actions are governed by a series of obligations and counterobligations.

Community integration on the basis of dyadic contracts shares the common characteristics of the classical kindred. Any unit has existence only in reference to a given ego. For every ego in the community the set of people with whom he maintains patterned interaction is different. Consequently, there is no basis for the formation of corporate groups founded on either kinship, compadrazgo, or friendship. Allegiances and alliances are crosscutting. No boundaries can be fixed to define a group of members and exclude nonmembers.

Gillin (1960: p. 29), like many writers before—scientific, philosophic, and popular—has commented on the individualistic orientation of Latin-American culture, of the high value placed on the worth of each single person in a society which is also characterized by a comparatively rigid class structure. The total society, like the family, is arranged into a series of separate, divided social roles hierarchically arranged. That one recognizes the intrinsic human value of every individual at the same time that one divides society into fixed social classes seems like a contradiction to Anglo-Americans, but, as Gillin points out, this is perfectly consistent from the Latin-American point of view. Tonaltecans see their community in just such a way.

Everyone in town is known by a nickname. Everyone is identified as having not only a social identity as an individual, but a social personality as well, a unique role in the community. Some of the nicknames refer to a physical trait: La Liebre for a tall, thin girl (The Rabbit), La Leona for someone with a leonine appearance, El Alfiler for an extremely slender woman (The Needle), La Gorda for a pear-shaped man (The Fat Woman), El Orejón (Big Ear), El Pando (Sway Back), El Molacho (The Gap-toothed One), El Zanate (The Blackbird). Other nicknames refer to personality traits: La Mula (The Mule), El Chango (The Monkey), El Terror, Siete Furias (Seven Furies), El Fantasma (The Ghost), La Muerte (Death) for someone considered stingy, while his brother was called Padre Eterno, El Músico for someone with a big appetite because proverbially musicians are big eaters, El Murciélago (The Bat). Some names refer specifically to behavior patterns not considered appropriate to the sex of the person named: La Arriera for a strong-minded, tough-speaking woman (The Muleteer), Lilí for one of the town homosexuals. The list is long and displays inventiveness, humor, and the hostility with which one customarily view's one's fellow man. Some of the nicknames are bequeathed in childhood; the origin of others is not clear. A few are remnants of outstanding incidents, as is the name of Valegrillos (Worth a Beetle). The man in question had a daughter who ran off with a married man known as El Soldado, even though he had never served in the military forces. One day when the father had had too much to drink, as was his almost daily custom, he ran up and down the street shouting, "Vale el grillo las relaciones de mi hija. La llevó un soldado" ("The relations of my daughter are worth a beetle. She was taken off by a soldier."). Afterwards the father became known as Valegrillos. The incident plays on the significance of nicknames in two ways: the origin of the father's name is explained and the nature of the abductor's nickname affects his social position and indirectly the honor of the girl.

Nicknames are clearly one of the mechanisms of informal social sanctioning. Certain kinds of nicknames may shame people into conforming to customary behavior patterns or punish people for failing to do so. In this way, they also support existing values and customary role behavior by defining acts or modes of acting that are considered deviant.

However, they have another effect, which is perhaps more long-lasting. When someone is first given a nickname, the sanctioning aspects are clearest. Novelty makes the disapproval effective, but in time the nickname becomes a signal, rather than a description or a form of ridicule. To refer to someone as La Arriera year after year means eventually that one accepts certain kinds of behavior as appropriate to a rather masculine woman. In time one assumes that The Clown jokes and The Mule is stubborn, for such is their nature. "Pues así son," informants say ("That's just the way they are").

The rules of etiquette and respect demand that an individual not be addressed by his nickname. For someone to answer to it is considered indelicate and *descarado* (lacking in face). Although there are a few exceptions (nicknames so generally used that they become accepted in lieu of a name or those which were given in early childhood and which the possessor has always answered to), these rules are usually followed. Nevertheless, individual behavior tends to be influenced by the nature of one's nickname, since most people know with what sobriquet they have been favored. Furthermore, the nickname affects the behavior of other people toward its owner. El Payaso tends always to be joked with because he is a clown and he is The Clown. Like Merton's self-fulfilling prophecy, the nickname helps shape the behavior it names.

Thus in a society which demands a high level of conformity in behavior there is a surprising tolerance of deviant individuals and deviant personalities. Nicknames become a mandate for individuals to be something else than the average Tonaltecan. There is a place in Tonalá for the lame, the halt, and the blind; for the sharp-tongued, the violent-tempered, the confused, and the feeble-minded.

The social structure of Tonalá can be seen as an interwoven and crosscutting web of dyadic alliances. In such a situation loyalties are often conflicting. One cannot join one's compadre in action for fear of finding oneself at odds with one's next-door neighbor or one's fellow association member. The Tonalá way out is to withdraw, to behave politely, to make no overt commitments.

IX. TO MAKE A LIVING

If one were to place a symbol for Tonalá on a pictorial map of Mexico, it would be of a pottery vessel. Pottery-making is the single most important feature of the town and constitutes its only source of fame and renown. Of the pottery-making towns and villages of Jalisco the cottage industry of Tonalá produces finer wares than any other. About half the households in town are supported by the making of clay jugs, cooking pots, and water bottles. These products are then distributed over much of Mexico, some of them eventually reaching discount houses in San Francisco, or New York gift shops.

Although the industry has a long history, it is impossible to determine whether Tonalá was a craft-specialized village at the time of the Conquest. Fray Antonio Tello retells in some detail Nuño de Guzmán's taking of Tonalá, describing a banquet given by the queen of the region in Nuño's honor at which there were set out pottery bowls filled with food (Tello, 1891). The friars upon whose accounts Tello draws had other interests than pottery, and we do not find out if the objects were made in that town or another. Nowhere is there any evidence that the village specialized in making pottery, just as there is no evidence to the contrary, for neither the Franciscan nor the Augustinian chronicler (Tello, 1945; Basalenque, 1886) mentions any introduction of new crafts into Tonalá by the monks attached to the church there. Some later historians have assumed that Tonalá specialized in pottery production before the Conquest, but this assumption seems to rest only on the fact that Tonalá and pottery have been inextricably related for as long as anyone can remember.

But if we cannot be sure of pottery as an industry in Tonalá in pre-Conquest times, by the mid-eighteenth century it was well established and obviously of some antiquity. Writing in 1742, Mota Padilla (1870: p. 44), who seldom had anything good to say about Indians, praised Tonalá pottery highly:

> Tonalá has mines of a clay so special that in all the world there is nothing similar, and for this reason there is so much esteem for their vases, jars, water jugs, urns, tankards, and various kinds of animal figures, large and small, so polished and perfect that in many parts of Europe women carry them as amulets, so soft are they as to aroma and taste that often women eat such clay; for this reason this ware is sold by *arrobas* [a Spanish measure of about twenty-five pounds] in Jalapa, Veracruz, and Acapulco even when it is broken; it is more esteemed than crystal, than china, and more than vases of Alcorza; that is, the very delicate things are. These can be enjoyed only in Guadalajara because of the difficulty of transporting them, and then [only] within the city. There are vessels so delicate and precious that [each piece is] worth

three silver *reales,* and it is not only because of the gilt that the price is so high, for it is only used for exports and for decorating secretaries and jars, of which one or another is made of such clay. If one puts water in the jars, especially in summer, they let off such an aroma that women are incited to eating earth and the dropsical to drinking. The same thing occurs in Guadalajara during the first rainstorms of the year when the earth gives off a similar aroma.

Both the Ceramic Museum in Tlaquepaque and the State Museum of History and Anthropology in Guadalajara own specimens of Tonalá ware that date from the seventeenth century. Isabel Marín (Marín de Paalen, n.d.: p. 16) says that available examples indicate a continuous production for the last three and a half centuries, but that the known pieces do not prove either an abundant early production or a great development of craftsmanship. This last phrase probably refers to the fact that once Tonaltecan pottery techniques had developed to a level sufficient to produce satisfactory and pleasing ceramics—a stage already reached by the seventeenth century, according to the evidence of extant pieces—there was neither much experimentation in the direction of developing other kinds of pottery nor much increase in technological competence.

In spite of the fact that the origin of pottery in Tonalá is not clear, there is no doubt that today the manufacturing of ceramics is the town's most important economic activity. Of the 859 households for which I have occupational data, 268, or 31 per cent, are supported only by pottery-making as a household industry. In 128 additional households more than one member makes pottery, although the family income is supplemented from other sources. The head of the house may also farm, or a family member may work as a dressmaker in town or as a mechanic in a city repair-shop. In 36 more households a single potter maintains his family, while in an additional 22 the income of one potter is supplemented by a family member working in farming, manufacturing, or services. Thus the income of 454 households (53 per cent) derives in part or entirely from pottery-making, an industry which in Tonalá in still overwhelmingly a family concern, for in 46 per cent of the households pottery-making is a family enterprise—even though there is a ceramic factory in town.

The clay used to make Tonalá ware comes from several sources. Just to the north of town is a good-sized mine of *barro colorado* (red clay) which is one of the two raw materials used in making cooking ware. Clays are also obtained from deposits near Tlaquepaque, Salatitán, Santa Cruz de las Huertas, and El Rosario. The latter is the source of the basic material for the common variety of water bottles, while the extra-fine ones are slipped with a *barro de olor* (aromatic clay) from Sayula, a town about a hundred miles away.

When a household has run out of clay, a man may take his burro and dig enough clay for a few days' work, or he may go with his sons and a couple of pack animals to get enough for a week or more. Increasingly, however, potters prefer buying clay delivered to their door. A man who is working on a large order or who manufactures items that require large quantities of clay finds it more economical to buy raw materials rather than spend the time mining them himself. Buying clay represents one of the few instances in which the potters economize by counting time as a commodity. It may be that the part-time specialty of clay-selling has developed because some of the nearby sources for special clays have run out. Consequently, merchants or farmers who own trucks or pickups often engage part time in fulfilling the transportation needs of the potters both in obtaining and transporting raw materials and in taking goods to market. Nevertheless, many potters still mine their own clay.

As is general in central Mexico, two or more clays are mixed together to produce a paste of the proper plasticity; temper as such is neither used nor understood.

Two basic textures of clay are recognized: *barro fuerte* or *pegajoso* (strong or sticky clay) and *barro suelto* (loose clay), a sandy substance. A little of the latter is added to a quantity of the former according to the potter's individual preference. The technical requirements of the craft set limits as to how sticky or how loose the mixture can be made, but there is enough leeway so that the mixing formulas are rather varied. Clay also comes in three colors: black, red, and white. Barro suelto is usually white, but pegajoso is either black or red, the former being used for toys, piggy banks, and some water bottles, whereas the latter is used for cooking pots which must withstand direct fire.

The tools and supplies used by Tonaltecan potters are few and simple: baskets for moving clay, wire screens, pieces of leather for shaping, stones for patting out paste into flat cakes, small pieces of sheet metal for slicing, cord or fiber for cutting even edges, brushes, rags, and burnishing tools.

Once the clay is in the home, it is spread out to dry in a sunny place such as the cobbled streets or stone sidewalks. When it is dry, and partially broken up by the passing traffic, it is gathered into handleless baskets (*chiquihuites*) and dumped in a corner of the house where the floor—of packed earth, stone, or cement—is smooth enough to provide a suitable surface for the grinding. The clay is pulverized by crushing it beneath large stones. The work is heavy and almost always done by men. This fine clay is passed through a wire screen to eliminate large lumps, and then enough water is added to wet a day's supply. The quantity dampened is not too crucial, however, for if all is not used, it can be kept damp until the next day or it can be allowed to dry and be crushed again. Since the paste is hand-molded, it is left comparatively dry, but it is kneaded and any small particles of hard rock or pieces of obsidian are picked out. The kneading, like the crushing, is man's work. The regular pattern is for the clay to be made into paste in the morning, often before early morning Mass, and then it is allowed to "rest" until after breakfast when the next step in the process is begun.

Flat cakes or paste are patted out and worked over or into molds, for both mushroom molds and vertical halves are used (cf. Foster, 1948b: pp. 357–358). The molds may be of pottery, but nowadays more frequently they are of plaster of paris. Open-mouthed vessels are finished off by smoothing the upper edge with the help of a small flap of wet leather. Sometimes a coil is used to form the collar, which is then smoothed and shaped with the leather piece. Narrow-mouthed vessels are constricted by patting with a small wooden paddle, using a ball of clay as an anvil. Necks of water bottles and pitchers are molded separately. Handles are made by shaping ropes of clay which are then attached to the vessel with the help of a little water, and flattened and smoothed between the fingers. If the object is formed over an inside mold (e.g., piggy banks), the paste is allowed to dry in the shade for a few minutes. Then the piece is sliced in two with a small piece of sheet metal, the mold is removed, and the seams are joined together by wetting and smoothing over with the fingers.

The objects are then set out in the sun to dry. The amount of drying time is variable, for it is affected by the humidity of the day and the size of the object. Sometimes drying proceeds too rapidly, and then the pottery cracks.

This risk becomes particularly great during the dry, windy days of March and April. At such times makers of large cooking pots or dyeing vats try to protect their wares by storing the vessels in the shade, turning them once or twice daily, and covering them with damp cloths.

After drying, the vessel is slipped to give it the base color. Cooking pots, casseroles, mugs, and common water bottles are covered with a red slip, piggy banks with *matiz* (a fine, white clay), and fine water bottles and other decorative pieces to be finished by burnishing, with the aromatic barro de olor, sometimes called *varniz* (varnish).

Decorating brings out all the artistic skill of the potters as well as their ability to improvise the arrangement of motifs to fit the size and shape of the vessel, while still retaining traditional styles. There are several kinds of decoration customarily used in Tonalá, but, in addition, some potters are adept and willing to try their hand at copying other patterns. Consequently, there have been periods in which Tonaltecan potters have turned out imitation majolica or objects decorated with the foreigners' view of what is typically Mexican: a sleeping peon with a sombrero, leaning against a prickly-pear cactus, or garish "Aztec" ware with geometric designs. In the last few years they have made some pieces with a kind of "Chinese" decoration that appeals to Guadalajara buyers. On these pieces Oriental dragons undulate against backgrounds of black or mottled Chinese red.

Fortunately, there is a large market for traditionally decorated ware. Most utilitarian vessels are very simply painted: the rim bears a band of dark brown interrupted here and there by a green or blue section and accented by groups of white strokes. Mugs are adorned with the same three or four colors, but there is a wide decorative band of simple flowers, girls' names, and geometric borders around the outside. *Bandera* (flag) ware, so called for its use of the green and white of the Mexican flag against a red background, is decorated with flowers, scrolls, and birds executed with flourishes of a fairly wide brush. *Petatillo* (little petate or mat, its name deriving from a finely crosshatched background), on the other hand, is done in fundamentally the same colors as utilitarian ware, but the motifs of flowers, birds, and animals are developed in much detail and with delicate execution, covering large parts of the surface of the vessel with intricate designs.

Aromatic ware (*loza de olor*) varies in background color from the kinds of pottery described above. After a first slip of a very light beige clay with a characteristic fresh aroma, the vessel is painted in black, using the same iron manganese pigment employed in the red-based wares. The designs in black are leaves, animals, and geometric borders. The vessel is then dipped again in the light-colored slip, so that the black areas take on a gray tint. Then, with a very fine brush, details in the leaves and borders are put on with black and white, and other figures are added, using these colors and several shades of a rather pink-toned red. The finished product is elaborately painted with deer, dogs, birds, flowers, and leaves. Sometimes the pieces are decorated with an over-all design of little flowers or scrolls in a pattern that is reminiscent of seventeeth-century Persian pottery; the Tonaltecans call this kind of painting *percal* (percale). Other styles are also differentiated: *floreado* (flowered) for the pieces decorated with flora and fauna in complicated curvilinear designs, and *encaje* (lace) for the style in which emphasis is placed on an elaboration of the geometric and scroll borders.

The Tonaltecans are most proud of loza de olor and petatillo ware. The former has a long historical tradition which local potters have become aware of because of the exhibitions of the State Ceramic Museum in Tlaquepaque. Consequently, the potters make an effort to maintain its authenticity by using locally mined earth pigments and working in traditional motifs. Nevertheless, the designs are constantly being modified in subtle ways, for the potters vie with one another in inventing improvements in execution. The product of this decade can be distinguished from its seventeenth- and eighteenth-century forebears by its elaboration of detail, its fine, feathery strokes, and a slight difference in the pink and beige colors. Some of the potters are conscious of the variation in color and are experimenting to try to capture the exact colors of the old pieces.

The barro de olor ware gets its polished surface from burnishing, rather than from glazing. The unbaked vessel is wet in small patches with a little piece of cloth attached to a short stick, for it is considered important not to wet one's hands while they are "heated from the work of burnishing." Many potters believe that those who make water bottles are likely to get pneumonia or arthritis because they get wet while they are overheated. They, like other Latin Americans, believe that working heats the body so that it is easily susceptible to chilling, for contact with cold and wet objects upsets the balance of "humors" within a warm body (cf. Foster, 1953b, on classification of "hot" and "cold" in Latin-American folk medicine). The picture conjured up is of large quantities of water being spilled over onto the burnisher, but in fact, he dips a rag brush into a couple of inches of water in a clay mug and carefully wets a square inch at a time.

The tool used for burnishing is a metal-shod stone, which originally came to Tonalá with the glaze, when it was sold in large chunks. It quickly replaced the iron pyrite burnishing tools which had been used previously. The old tools had been suitable for polishing both concave and convex surfaces, whereas the new ones could only be used on convex surfaces. Nevertheless, the new burnisher-glazer-grinder was far superior technologically, and the old stones were completely abandoned. Vessels made from then on were polished on convex surfaces only. Eventually the industrial firms of Monterrey began marketing a preground glaze. An unforeseen result of this practice is that Tonalá potters are deprived of their source of burnishing tools—nor can they go back to using the old burnishers, for they have long since been lost. There is no local source of the hard material required, and no other object has come to hand which can be adapted for the purpose. In the meanwhile, a large demand for burnished pottery makes it unlikely that the technique will be abandoned. The potters are carefully hoarding their polishers until the day someone invents a new burnisher. The need for the new tool exists, but thus far no innovator has come forth to fill the gap.

After polishing, the barrio de olor ware is ready for its one firing. Glazed ware, however, is fired twice. After the first firing, it is covered with a thin layer of *greta* (glaze), lead oxide purchased in pulverized form from one of the several grocery stores handling potters' supplies. Each potter makes a mixture of this greta and *liga* (locally mined white rock), having learned through experience the proper proportions and consistency of the solution of greta, liga, and water. If the mixture is not right, colors run together, and the glaze will run or perhaps peel off the vessel. Even experienced potters have occasional failures.

Tonalá kilns are beehive shaped and made of bricks or adobes which eventually bake into light-colored brick as a result of use. The adobes are smaller than those used in house construction and are tapered toward one side so that they fit together neatly to form a smooth-surfaced cylinder.

A small door in the side opens to the firebox, which is separated from the chamber above by a grate. A central crown of bricks, known as a *corazón* (heart), supports shallow arches formed out of the pottery pipe made in the nearby village of Santa Cruz. Over this grate is placed a layer of potsherds arranged so as to form a well-covered, overlapped base which will protect the pottery above from the flaming fuel below. The pottery to be fired is stacked on the grate. Makers of fine ware use racks of clay and little tripod dividers called *caballos* (horses) to separate vessels, but inexpensive pieces are stacked against each other. In the loading of the kiln, one tries to arrange the pieces so that the heat will circulate evenly, so that as little contact as possible is made between glazed areas—for at such points the objects stick together—and so that the load is evenly balanced over the grate. Occasionally accidents occur. Part of the load may not be heated properly, and the colors come out wrong or the glaze runs off, large patches may have to be covered where objects were stuck together and had to be pulled apart, or a whole kilnful of pottery may collapse into the firebox. The latter kind of accident occurs fairly infrequently—we knew of only one case in 1959–1960—but when it does occur, it is a serious financial matter for the family. Finally large potsherds are placed over the stacked pottery, so that it is completely covered and protected from contact with the cool outside air.

The first firing of glazed ware (which occurs before glazing) and the only firing of loza de olor require comparatively low temperatures. Isabel Marín (Marín de Paalen, n.d.: p. 30) notes that the temperature in the first case is only 600° centigrade and in the second 850°. In the second firing of glazed ware the kiln is brought to a temperature of 900° C. However, these precise figures obscure the fact that the Tonaltecan potter has only limited control of the temperature of his kiln. He knows that in the firing of glazed ware higher temperatures are necessary, and he has a great deal of practical experience as to the amount of fuel necessary for the different kinds of baking in his own kiln. The other factor that must be taken into account, however, is the difficulty of obtaining fuel. Long ago all surrounding hills were stripped of hardwood trees. The potter must now make do with whatever he can: odds and ends of lumber bought from suppliers who have picked up scrap wood in the city, dry bushes and branches he himself gathers in the fields, or dry cow dung he buys from Tonalá's gatherers. Sometimes one of these vendors of fuel may take the risk of cutting branches or trees in the forested areas farther away, but he must then avoid the forestry inspectors along the highways and keep to back trails when bringing in the wood. Sawdust is used on occasion, while eucalyptus leaves brought from a stand of trees about ten miles away are considered a particularly good fuel for the second firing of glazed ware. Given the variety of fuel used, it is difficult for the potter to do more than *tantear* (estimate) how hot his oven is.

After firing, the pottery is allowed to cool in the covered kiln—usually overnight—and then as it is unloaded it is inspected for imperfections. Small breaks can sometimes be mended, and places where the glaze has pulled off can be covered by paint. If the flaws are too obvious, the pieces will be sold in the plaza for whatever price they can bring.

Most potters sit cross-legged on the floor or ground, sometimes with a burlap sack under them; before beginning to work they take off their shoes or sandals, for it is uncomfortable to work in this position while shod. Women may sit cross-legged with their skirts pulled down around them modestly, but most of them prefer a sidesaddle posture. Occasionally pottery makers sit in low chairs; only one family that I know of worked at a regular table height. The head of this family is one of the leaders in the pottery community, a shareholder in the local electric company, and collector and meter reader for this company. He is also president of the organized *Padres de Familia* (the parent group of the local federal school). At the suggestion of his wife, a woman of exceptional energy and intelligence, he improvised three work tables made of slabs of flat rock supported variously by piles of bricks and a tree stump. She preferred sitting in a chair to work, for she felt that sitting on the cold floor was harmful and made her feel stiff; she also said it gave her calluses on the sides of her feet to work sitting cross-legged. What she did not mention, but what I am sure was also an important factor in her urging her husband on to this "innovation," is the general feeling among city people and Tonaltecans alike that to work on the floor is demeaning. Most Tonaltecans, however, feel that they have no choice, for to make pottery is their *destino* (destiny), and one makes pottery seated on the floor.

Just as the houses of Tonalá do not provide work areas and facilities specifically adapted to pottery manufacture, neither do they provide space for storing materials. Clay is dried in the middle of the cobbled streets or on the stone sidewalks; thus, on the one hand, advantage is taken of the passage of vehicles and pedestrians to help crush it, but, on the other hand loss is permitted of considerable amounts from wind and dispersal between the stones. A side effect of this custom is the gradual building up of clay over the cobbles, so that in the rainy season the streets are muddy and in the dry season the wind carries large amounts of dust.

Since the supply of fuel is almost always less than the demand, one would expect the potters to stockpile fuel whenever they can get it at a reasonable price—particularly before the rainy season sets in and makes it almost impossible to use small branches and cow dung. Tonaltecans do not do so, however. In the first place, they neither own nor do they build shelter or shed to keep fuel dry. In the second place, since their economic orientation is toward spending or refraining from spending in reference to a long-term goal, they buy only the small quantities of fuel which will burn the week's supply of pottery.

One Sunday, for instance, while I was visiting the Ramírez family, a boy arrived with a donkey-load of cow dung. "A fine time for you to appear," said Pablo. "Everything is already fired. Yesterday when we needed fuel you didn't come around." The boy took his load and went off. Pablo explained to me that he had spent most of Saturday trying to buy fuel; finally by late afternoon he found some. He did not, however, buy any from the boy even though he was planning to fire pottery again on Wednesday and would have the same fuel-hunting problem again.

Saturday is traditionally one of the days for firing; on that afternoon, through most of the year, donkeys loaded with eucalyptus leaves would pass my door on their way to the barrio of the makers of *ollas* (cooking pots). It is about a twenty-mile round trip to obtain this fuel, but it is made every week, for no one stores a supply to last through several firings. Given this system of buying, the potters rely on traditional social ties to try to insure themselves against an absolute fuel famine: fuel-purchasing does not operate through an open competitive market, but through one's ties to a relative, a compadre, a barrio member. If one looks into the matter further, it becomes clear that if fuel were sold on the open market, the shortage of supply would force the price up—probably beyond the price which the potters could afford to pay, since they are not in a position to raise the selling price of their wares to any degree (see discussion of relationship of pottery and middlemen).

This lack of tools, of rationally organized work space, of facilities for storing materials, does not result from either disinterest or ignorance, but rather from the goals and expectations of the particular kind of economy the Tonaltecans participate in. One does not think in terms of loss of man-hours because of poor arrangements for work, for one assumes that hard work is a virtue of its own, and one makes one's economies in terms of short-term goals. Eustolia gave me an illustration of this point of view and how it operated in the household. She said both her mother and her aunts are accustomed to making a fire for the tortilla *comal* (griddle) out of green wood and getting it started with the coal from a single cigarette. Her father insists that his daughters should learn this trick because it is the sign of a truly economical housewife to borrow her husband's cigarette, take one or two puffs off it and light the fire. Eustolia, however, who belongs to a sector of the younger generation which has had more contact with the city, feels that the practice is a false economy. "To save a match one loses a whole morning." The statement is of particular interest for it indicates that she is thinking of time as a commodity. However, although she thinks of time as having economic importance, she does so mainly in reference to housework, for her experiences in the city were in this area. She learned that time is money in housework in the city, for she was earning money as a maid. The idea of the value of time does not automatically carry over into pottery-making, for in this area Eustolia and Tonaltecans in general feel that the city has nothing to teach them.

An observer watching pottery being made finds it difficult to generalize about the organization of work. Ordinarily things run smoothly; everyone seems to know what to do next; few orders are given. Since few conflicts about pottery-making come out in the open, it is difficult for an outsider to decide upon what basis roles are assigned and how decisions are made. The seeming freedom in performance and role definition is pushed into apparent amorphism by the fact that the work group can consist of a dozen persons or of only one, since the production unit is the household and household composition varies greatly. The number of workers varies from one house to the next and also from one hour to the next within a household, for pottery-making does not necessarily take precedence over other kinds of activity during the work day. Among families whose pottery-making I observed, there were households of a man and wife alone; of three unmarried brothers working with a married brother, his wife, and his mother-in-law; of typical patrilocal extended families; of nuclear families; of extended and nuclear families plus a hired hand or two; of a three-generation family including both sons and daughters and in-marrying males and females. Given this kind of variety in work groups, it becomes a delicate matter to separate out the principles upon which action is taken and roles are played.

The most obvious organizational principle is that of the division of labor by barrios. Traditionally, Cuartel 1 makes water jugs and decorative ware; this part of town is nicknamed Tateposquillo (for little Tatepozco, a nearby village that produces *cántaros,* large undecorated water jars). In Cuartel 2 water jugs are also made; in addition, in this barrio most piggy banks and toys are made. Cuartel 3 has a high proportion of full-time farmers. Most of the potters in this area make simple mugs. The Fourth Cuartel is the center for cooking ware of all kinds. These divisions are not rigid, of course. There are piggy-bank makers in

Cuartel 3 and makers of mugs in Cuartel 1, but on the whole, people in the eastern half of town do not make unglazed water jugs and those in the western part do not make cooking ware.

This situation would be a classically simple case of organic solidarity if the townspeople were selling primarily to each other; another kind of interdependence is created, however, by the fact that the community as a whole provides outside buyers with a wide range of ceramic commodities. In other words, a buyer can come to Tonalá and at the established market on Thursdays and Sundays select from a large variety of pottery. The existence of the institutionalized market depends upon the tacit agreement of all the sellers as to when and where items will be sold. The interdependence of the potters from various barrios is a little less clear in respect to selling to wholesalers, for there need be no inter-Tonaltecan agreement or understanding in these cases. The terms and circumstances of the contracts between buyer and seller are then the result of bargaining between the two parties.

There is a growing tendency toward another kind of specialization in the Tonalá pottery industry. As the market for wares widens, and the vagaries of the fashions and fads of the national market impinge on Tonalá, there are constant demands for new shapes of vessels and new kinds of decorations. This kind of pressure has made some potters turn to other specialists in some phases of production. For instance, several men are known as specialists in making molds and in inventing new shapes. According to the legendary history of Cuartel 2, about the time of World War I the pottery market was very poor. It is said that only one shape of *botellón* (water bottle) was known—the classic round body with a long straight neck. Zacarías Jimón decided that perhaps if he had an assortment of objects to offer for sale, he could sell more; after some experimenting, he made molds for several new shapes. In a travel book written in 1939 (Oglesby, 1939: pp. 155–156) Jimón's pottery is described: "Frequently they [the pottery vessels] are taller, more graceful and truly classical in their restraint. . . . The work of Jimón approaches more nearly the vertical shape preferred by the Greeks. That is, the object is tall and slender rather than low and broad." Jimón invented a shape he calls a *granada* (pomegranate). This particular vessel is molded only in his household; several other potters buy unfired ware from him and paint and fire it themselves. This kind of specialization—molding or painting—is not done on a strictly cooperative basis; the painter buys the molded pieces from another potter; he then sells the finished product to the wholesaler.

There exists a variation of this kind of specialization; a single potter or the head of a pottery-making household may agree to deliver certain quantities of unfired ware to the factory or to another household which cannot mold enough ware to fulfill its contracts. Although this procedure seems identical with household specialization, it is a development similar to wage labor. In these cases the maker of the unfired ware is not a designer, nor is he considered to be a specialist because of particular aptitude; he is rather in the position of a pieceworker in a cottage industry, for he provides the manufacturer-entrepreneur with partly finished goods at a set price; what he makes and how much is paid is decided by the man to whom he delivers his pottery. According to one informant, this practice is of fairly recent origin; this informant, an elderly middle-class lady who had herself been a wholesale dealer in pottery, claims that the rise of this practice has been responsible for low motivation toward work among the potters producing unfired ware, for they do not feel responsible for the quality of work nor do they feel impelled to run off more than a standard daily production based on what can be made in a minimum day. The lady may have been mourning the dear, gone golden days when labor was cheap and hours were long, for the degeneration of recent times is a favorite theme of hers, but there is no doubt that a piecework system does not favor high-quality work.

Division of labor according to sex and age is by no means inflexible and unambiguous. Certain kinds of jobs are considered to be men's work and others to be within the province of women, generally speaking, but the rules are not ironclad and none of the pottery activities are forbidden to anyone because of sex. Ordinarily men mine clay either as individuals or as a family group of father and sons or a group of brothers. Grinding and mixing clay is heavy work and is usually done by a man. If the household contains several adult males, one of the young, strong men ordinarily takes on this job. Firing the pottery is also a man's job, but the women help to load and unload the kiln. On the other hand, in families where burnished ware is made, it is almost always the women who do the polishing. Other jobs are not clearly delegated to one sex or the other, although general tendencies can be seen. Large pieces are almost always molded by men, a fact that would seem to be related only to the greater physical strength of males, were it not for the other fact that in a family making only medium-sized objects men will turn out the larger of the pieces. Men tend to make the objects that are considered the important ones and to work on the processes that are thought to be essential in the context of the kind of pottery made in each particular household.

Insofar as the division of labor according to age is concerned, two factors enter in. Children, since they are both less skilled and less prestigious than adult males, routinely perform tasks that are easier and mold objects that are smaller; often they do women's pottery jobs, although small boys do not ordinarily do any other kinds of women's work. Nevertheless, boys must learn to be adult potters and consequently must get experience in all the processes of pottery-making. By the time they are about fourteen they have tried their hand at grinding and preparing clay and at helping with the firing. Since it is usually assumed that girls will eventually marry out of the family, there is less emphasis placed on training them in all phases of production. Occasionally individual girls show unusual talent; in such cases they are encouraged to develop their skills in molding and painting. There are a few women in Tonalá who are famous as potters in their own right.

If a woman marries a man outside her own barrio, she usually has to learn to make a different kind of pottery. On the whole the techniques are similar enough so that there is no real problem of having to learn new motor habits and new processes, and the changeover can be relatively smooth so far as the technical aspects are concerned. Sometimes a woman may decide to stop making pottery when she moves to her new home—either because she dislikes the work itself or because she finds the new production unit an uncongenial social group. She may find it difficult to adjust to the way things are done in the new house in general, but she cannot withdraw from participating in the housework, whereas she sometimes can drop out of pottery-making. This problem of adjusting to the new household is, of course, much more difficult when one is living in an extended family rather than alone in a house with a new husband.

A pottery production unit is not a factory. Work does not proceed uninterruptedly within a set working day.

The hour for beginning is not always the same; ordinarily a man arises early—in the dimness before dawn or at cock's crow—so the clay can be mixed with water before attending the *misa de alba* (dawn Mass) held at six o'clock. In many households one does not resume working until after breakfast, a meal usually eaten between eight and nine. Work proceeds until dinner, somewhere around two or three, resumes at about four after a period of relaxation, and continues until it is too dark to see well. This arrangement makes a long day and also means that the major pottery-makers of the family put in from about eight to ten hours of work apart from the long meal intervals. The work periods are often interrupted, however.

Certain activities take precedence over pottery-making—farming, for example. Most ceramic operations can be postponed or relegated to some other member of the family, while for plowing, seeding, and harvesting, time is often a most crucial factor. If there is conflict between the fulfillment of a pottery contract and the immediate need to perform a farming task, the former is allowed to slide. Pottery dealers are accustomed to this fact and, although they may urge potters to complete an order, during the rainy season (the major agricultural season) they have come to expect delays in the delivery of pottery.

Ceremonial activities also take precedence over pottery manufacture. Attendance at weddings, funerals, and the fiestas accompanying baptisms and confirmations are seen as obligations; it is not considered a valid excuse to say, "I had work to do and did not have time to come." Regular Church holidays, of course, are days on which one does not work; one also refrains from working in order to participate in the rites and ceremonies associated with the religious societies to which one belongs.

Women interrupt their work as potters to perform

household tasks, for they are wives and mothers primarily and pottery makers secondarily. They do not begin working on pottery until the house and patio have been swept, breakfast has been eaten, and the shopping done for dinner. Marketing in Tonalá is not a simple matter, however, and the morning is constantly disjointed by trips to the plaza or to the corner store or to the tortillería to get a pinch of this or a handful of that for the afternoon meal. Small children are, as for housewives everywhere, another constant source of interruption. Infants in Tonalá are treated with almost immediate attention toward their needs; toddlers may make demands on their mother's time to obtain food or for momentary comforting, but she continues working while she distracts them with a few words or by offering them a piece of clay or some bright scrap of cloth to play with. As the children grow older, their needs are less likely to take precedence over the father's need of the mother's help as pottery maker. By the time the child is of school age the mother will no longer stop bringing dry vessels for the father to paint when the child is crying; she is more likely to tell him to stop making such a racket.

Nowadays school provides the major interruption in the child's workday. Not everyone of school age attends school, of course; nor are there facilities if everyone should decide to attend. In 1960 the federal school in town had a fluctuating enrollment centering somewhere around 500, and the parish school had another 30 or so pupils. Pottery family households comprise 31 per cent of the total number of households in town, and they alone have at least 400 children of school age. Nevertheless one can infer that going to school for boys was considered less important in the past than was producing pottery, for out of 268 pottery families, in 147 the head of the household is illiterate.

One cannot, of course, assume that all of the above sources of interruption of work are of equal order. There are, on the one hand, activities that are considered of immediate urgency. But emergencies are culturally defined at least in part. While in the United States a woman working at home typing envelopes or making telephone solicitations might let her husband make his own lunch, in Tonalá a woman would always set aside the pot she is working on in order to serve her husband a meal. For a man who is a part-time farmer (a secondary occupation from the observer's point of view), going out to weed a field is considered enough of an emergency for him to let a pottery contract lapse.

On the other hand, there are activities which are not assumed to be emergencies, but which take priority because they are considered more important. Ceremonial activities and participation in festivals take precedence when a choice is to be made between working and going to a wedding or to Mass. The view of Tonaltecan life as one unending round of fiestas because of the villagers' laziness and preference for partying is not only patronizing, but untruthful, although it is the kind of response one gets from most Tonaltecans when one asks why someone is not working on a particular day. This kind of ranking of activities comes about because in the Tonaltecan social universe ceremonies and rites are important aspects of the ties and obligations which allow a Tonaltecan society to exist at all. It is not that the party-going villager does not realize that bread must be earned by working, but that he knows certain kinds of obligations are of primary importance if he does not intend to live the life of a hermit.

Within the pottery production unit itself the father or oldest male is responsible for making decisions involved with pottery-making. He is the one who undertakes an agreement to deliver a certain amount of pottery to a dealer, and he is the one who buys clay, pigment, and fuel. The family head referred to here is the head of the nuclear, not the extended, family. In a patrilocal family each nuclear unit contracts for, makes, and markets its own products. If a son works with his father before he is married, all the income from the joint enterprise goes directly to the father; the son receives in return spending money and clothing. After marriage, it is customary for the new family to produce its own pottery even when it exists within a patrilocal household. The firing is done cooperatively since ordinarily there is only one kiln per household, and it is used on the days preceding market days. All participating nuclear families are expected to contribute toward the purchasing of fuel although the senior family head usually does the actual buying. If the head of the household dies leaving a widow and grown children behind, one of the sons takes over the economic responsibility—an adult unmarried son by preference. If the only adult son is already married, then he must assume economic responsibility, although the mother and the unmarried children are likely to continue making pottery independently. If they do so, then they keep their income separate from that of the married son and his family.

Although the formal locus of authority is comparatively clear, Tonaltecans do not live under the kind of patripotestal system anthropologists are familiar with in Africa. In many contexts the father does not speak for his family in making a decision, and in many contexts members of the family make individual decisions. As has been mentioned above, a woman may refuse to make pottery; she may contract separately to make extra items or she may occasionally produce a few dozen mugs or toys to be sold on the plaza. Ordinarily she undertakes these independent economic activities only when she has accomplished what her husband expects of her in the family production unit, but most husbands feel that it is up to her to decide what to do with this extra income. Frequently she has it earmarked for some special thing—shoes for a child or a special contribution to one of the religious associations she belongs to.

Ideally speaking, the nuclear family is a pottery-making *group,* but in actuality the group qualities of the family are weakly developed. In the first place, the lines of internal differentiation of the production unit are not clear-cut, although there are a few general regularities of activities based upon sex and age as set forth previously. Secondly, since the lines of internal differentiation of roles are not clear, so the mutual interdependence pattern is not clear either. The work could be arranged so that each member of the group is responsible for the manufacturing of entire vessels with cooperative endeavor on those parts where it would be economically more feasible (e.g., obtaining clay and firing, as well as marketing). If one asks a Tonaltecan how the pottery work is organized, the above is often the description he will give you; it is what they think they do, but actual observation modifies this view. The other possible kind of organization would be the rationalization of the process through some kind of assembly-line procedure. Again if one asks a Tonaltecan, one is likely to get an answer that that is exactly what they do, since there are times when certain steps of the production are taken over by one or more members of the family to the exclusion of others, who then work on other steps. But again observation reveals that this is not what they do—not even in the factory.

From the outsider's point of view it looks as if the

pottery-making, like housekeeping, buying, and preparing for fiestas, is not organized in reference to the final goal as a long-term or even medium-range project. No one, for instance, estimates how much work the family can produce in a month and then plans the work and acquires supplies accordingly. Work is done *ad hoc.* The father, the formal decision-maker, does not coordinate the efforts of the members of the production unit, and each member makes many small decisions about when to begin, when to stop, how many units to make during a work period, and so forth. Such an informal system would seem to be unworkable if it were not for two major factors which grease the wheels of production. First, Tonaltecans seldom produce the maximum amount that they could make, even without technological improvements. Since the completion of any given job is seldom urgent, and wholesalers almost never apply formal sanctions to force the prompt delivery of goods contracted for, the number of decisions that need to be made about pottery production are kept at a minimum. Once the family head has made an agreement to produce a certain kind and a certain amount of pottery, the daily decisions about how to work can be left to the individual worker; there is only limited need for the coordination of effort, for the margin of time allowed for nonproductive activities, given the amount of production contracted for, is large by the standards of an engineered productive system. On occasions when the head of the family takes on a commitment to deliver a large amount of pottery, and either because he needs a certain sum of money immediately or because he is obligated to the pottery dealer in some way, must deliver the goods within a limited time period, the supervision of work must be much closer. Then one finds the father giving verbal commands and assigning family members to specific tasks.

In the second place, the looseness of organization is also workable because the production unit is the family unit. It is of paramount importance in a "traditional" or proto-industrial production system of the kind one finds in Tonalá pottery-making that one learn the economic role as part of the socialization process. This kind of learning begins very early, from the time the child is first aware of the activities of other family members. He learns to perform gradually, with daily increases in skill, over a very long period of time as compared with how he would learn a job in a city factory. Consequently, the modes of working of the members of the production unit become highly routinized and peculiar to each family. The idiosyncratic character of the organization of work in each production unit as compared with the method of production, which is generally similar throughout Tonalá, makes it difficult for the observer to see more than vague outlines of the division of labor and to generalize about it.

This overlap of production and socialization units has other results also. It puts a high premium on the traditional modes of operation, for in part the smoothness of the functioning of the production unit depends on everyone doing what he usually does. Deviation from this course by the younger family members—who are the most likely ones to be interested in trying something new—threatens the authority of the older members not only in their roles as foremen and superintendents of production, but as father or older brother. This kind of threat is too disruptive to be allowed to be carried through very often. Consequently, father must know best, not only as father, but also as head pottery-maker.

The second result of this situation is that rewards and punishment for performance in the economic sphere come in forms other than as economic sanctions. A son who consistently turns out substandard pottery may be beaten, but he is unlikely to be punished by a cutting-down on his food or by a refusal to buy him a shirt. This is the reverse of the frequent practice in the United States, where economic sanctions are applied to children for nonperformance in other spheres of activity; the child's allowance may be cut because he was heard using profanity, for instance. In Tonalá rewards for economic performance do not ordinarily come as simple economic rewards. They are a by-product of an increased income for the family as a whole. Learning to be a good potter makes one an admired and respected person; but it does not lead directly to owning luxuries or to eating better. Consistently throughout Tonalá life there is this de-emphasis of economic rewards and a consequent de-emphasis of economic goals in preference to another goal—that of being a respected person—which can be attained by other means than performance in an economic role.

Occasionally wage labor is employed in the household pottery units. If a family has a rush order or one larger than it can handle, someone may be hired temporarily to help out. This person is assigned work by the family head, but on the whole he works as if he were a member of the family. There is some loss of efficiency in using hired labor, for the hired man's presence is intrusive in an organization in which work is carried on with little direction or supervision. Nevertheless, this fact is often offset by the smaller number of interruptions in his work, for as long as he is in another's house, he is acting out his economic role primarily. In his own house occasions often arise in which his roles as father, potter, farmer, man, Catholic, member of an association, and compadre are in conflict.

These wage laborers are frequently members of other household production units which are in a slack period, or they are drawn from the ranks of people who are marginal in the Tonalá production system: braceros who have returned from the United States for a short trip and are out of funds, unmarried male adults who have quarreled with the head of their family, or former potters who have some other primary occupation but want to earn some cash. Such employment is functionally specific, and does not entail other kinds of social obligations. For instance, one need not attend the baptismal party for an employer's child if one only knows him in the context of this kind of employment. However, ordinarily one also knows him as neighbor or kinsman, so one goes anyway. Similarly, one hires potters, not compadres, but one tends to draw a worker from the neighborhood because communication with other cuarteles is less well-developed than within one's own.

A community study with no time-depth cannot, of course, indicate the rate at which wage labor is growing in importance as compared with household industries. One can, however, state that at the present time the wage laborer occupies a comparatively small role in the total pottery production of the town. These workers are employed temporarily and casually; the one other exception during the year I spent there was the workshop operated under the direction of one of the men from the Ceramic Museum in Tlaquepaque. Sometimes a young man may work for wages while employed as an apprentice in a household unit, but the tie is usually established on the basis of kinship bonds; one is apprenticed to a relative if one must go outside the immediate family in order to learn the skill, and if one is to accept an apprentice, one prefers a relative of some kind to reveal one's secrets to. There is no regular mother's brother-teacher complex; the choice of relative to whom one is to be apprenticed depends upon who needs an extra hand to help with the work rather than upon a preference for any particular kin status.

One of the first things that strikes the eye of the visitor to the town is a large billboard at the entrance announcing the Aldana Pottery Factory in letters four feet high and in English. Since it is the only advertisement in town, one is given the mistaken impression that the factory dominates production, that Tonalá is a one-factory town, a smaller version of Weirton or Steubenville. However, the Aldana factory occupies a different kind of position.

About thirty years or so ago the present owner of the factory, who was living in Guadalajara at that time, began buying pottery that Tonaltecan potters brought to the market of San Juan de Dios. For several generations one of the major outlets for Tonalá pottery had been at that market, the villagers bringing in a week's production on donkeys. City people still go to the Libertad Market (on the site of San Juan de Dios) to buy pottery, but most of the pottery is now sold at permanent booths by middlemen who have bought their goods in Tonalá and Tlaquepaque. Occasionally someone takes a basket-load of mugs or water bottles on the bus to sell directly in the city, but the Libertad Market is no longer a major outlet.

Thirty years ago the situation was different. The potter would take his goods to town, lay out his wares in the street area to the north of the old market, and trade and haggle with the housewives who came to buy cooking pots and water bottles. Sometimes at the end of the day he was left with a basket-load or so that he had been unable to sell. Rather than carry the load home again he sold it for a low price to owners of permanent booths or to other individuals engaging in small speculations. According to the villagers, Sr. Aldana began his pottery ventures in this way

—buying up tag ends of goods and then selling them at other markets in the city. In any case, he is not a native of Tonalá and began in the marketing rather than the production end of the industry. Eventually he set up the factory and settled in the town.

On an average the factory employs about twenty people although the number fluctuates seasonally from ten to thirty. Much of the ware produced is of traditional Tonalá type—both cooking and ornamental ware—but souvenir items for Sr. Aldana's retail shop in Tlaquepaque and for gift shops at the United States border are also made. The techniques of manufacturing are identical with those of the household production units except that a potter's wheel is used as a turntable for finishing off all large vessels, the kilns are larger, and loading is made somewhat easier by the use of racks.

Both men and women are hired, and in general the division of labor is similar to that described above: men mix clay and mold large pieces, and women mold small pieces and burnish. Both men and women paint and apply glaze. The factory also hires men to drive trucks and to help load, both men and women packing pottery for transport.

The factory is a paleotechnic one in some ways—to use Mumford and Geddes's phrase (Mumford, 1934). There is little attention paid to making a good physical working environment: no artificial lighting is provided, and the painters work under a sheltered area where the light is like the dusk inside a cave; the floors are earthen and uneven so that during the rainy season one has to skirt around puddles; one working area is uncomfortably near the heat of the kilns. Nevertheless, the conditions are neither better nor worse than they are in the cottage industry.

The way in which work is organized and the pace at which it proceeds is also much like that in the household industry. Interruptions are allowed to some extent, and there is little use of authority to push a particular rate of production. However, since most of the workers are paid on a piecework basis, they tend to set their own rates according to their need and their motivation toward money. Wages as a goal are only part of the picture in reference to pace of work; traditional *tareas* (tasks) are also important.

All pottery production in Tonalá—within the factory and without—is tied to the concept of tarea, the task or chore to be accomplished according to traditional requirements of what constitutes a day's work. Most potters will quit working when this amount has been done, unless they feel immediate and extreme pressure to finish an order. To complete a traditional tarea, one need not reorganize one's work habits in order to make production more efficient, nor need one push oneself every moment of the time. Consequently, there is an air of relaxation and ease about the work of the potters that is most appealing to anyone who has worked in a factory with an assembly line or a speedup system. The Aldana factory has this same air of people working busily, but not frantically. Workers in the factory always have the alternative of working at home if they are pushed too hard or if they have disagreements with the foreman. The factory does manage to hold a core of skilled potters, but there is always some turnover in the labor force, for differences of opinion arise even in a comparatively easy atmosphere. The disagreements are sometimes with the management, often with fellow workers, but rarely with the owner himself.

On the whole the operation runs without obvious difficulties in production. Pots are molded, dried, painted, and fired day after day without snarls, and one begins to assume that the Tonalá way of organizing work is somehow the natural way and that for pots to be made they must be made in this way. There do exist, however, other possible ways of organizing the work, although these kinds of work organization are seldom employed in Tonalá.

Any way of arranging a work pattern must take into account the technological requirements of the manufacturing process. Certain things must be done first: clay must be mixed before it is molded—and at some points relatively fixed quantities of time must be allowed unless one raises the technological level—and pots must be allowed to dry a certain amount of time regardless of one's need for hurrying. Nevertheless, there are areas of action in which alternatives do exist. If one is only concerned with the goal of turning out the most ware while personnel and tools remain the same, there are two principal ways of organizing work that will economize time in such a way as to increase output.

By the first method, units of work are divided so that the objects being produced move from one work space to another in a regular pattern so as to keep the time spent in handling the objects at a minimum, to concentrate tools where they are used, and to simplify the flow of objects. By this method the work area is divided into spaces that coincide with the technological processes. Thus, there would be either in home or factory a clay-mixing area, a molding area, a drying area, a painting area, a firing area, and the movement of partially completed objects would be unidirectional. A partly rational arrangement of this kind in the homes is broken up by the fact that most areas are multipurpose, for they must be used also for eating, visiting, washing dishes, and children's play areas. In addition, areas for drying and mixing clay are in most households poorly adapted for this purpose. In the factory there are spaces which are somewhat more functionally specific, but little attention is paid to the smooth flow of objects as they are processed, so that from the point of view of someone concerned with productive efficiency much time is lost as cups, ashtrays, and casseroles are carried back and forth, in and out, around and about.

The other possible way of organizing units of work would be on the basis of time and interlocking performance of steps in the process. In this procedure the molding process, for instance, would be broken up into steps. These steps would then be assigned to individuals in units and the work force distributed in such a way that the object could be completed through integrated cooperative effort. During the time I was in the field, there was one attempt to try this kind of thing in Tonalá. An agent from a Los Angeles wholesaler came to town and placed a large order with the Sánchez brothers, who specialize in burnished decorative ware. The order was unusually large, and the dealer was interested in having it completed as soon as possible. When the work was not forthcoming in the amount of time the agent felt was reasonable (and unknown to him, some of the ware they were producing for him they were selling to others), he suggested to the oldest brother that more work could be turned out if they set up an assembly line to do the molding. A few extra hands were hired, and a plan devised with the help of the buyer.

The day I went to watch this innovation the molding team was making pigeons. The body of the bird was formed in two halves, the bottom half made by one person, the top by another; a third person joined the pieces together and added a neck and head which had been made by a fourth member of the team. The process did not go smoothly. The two young women laughed and giggled, each team member was less particular about how well made his own section of the bird was, and no one member felt responsible for the finished product. Several of the pigeons fell apart and had to be made over. A few days later I visited this household again. No assembly line was in sight. The oldest brother explained that the method had not worked out: the finished pottery was not up to the standard of a Sánchez product, and they were not able to produce more with the assembly line than they were by their usual method.

A factor which he did not mention, but which bears on the question as to why the Tonaltecans, some of whom are familiar with assembly-line factories in Guadalajara and the United States, do not adapt this method of working to pottery production, is that of the short-term contracts made with the middleman. Usually the work is contracted for week by week. Such a system does not allow a potter to collect a large enough sum of money at one time to help tide him over while his new production system is going through its initial shakedown phase. As he sees it, he cannot afford to take the financial risk of trying a new kind of organization.

From our point of view the assembly-line method has the advantage of turning out more items in a given amount of time with a given number of workers. Tonaltecans both in home and factory feel that by their traditional methods they are already producing as much as they can. In addition, even if one could prove to them that they could increase production through this means, they feel that the losses that would accompany this system would outweigh the benefits, for quality would be sacrificed. Perhaps to the individual potter the most important loss would be that of his control over what he is doing, of the flexibility of his use of time. In the traditional system he decides when to begin and when to stop (even in the factory he has this choice to some extent). If he decides to take a day off or to plant a corn crop, the production unit need not come to a halt. In what to us is a rational and efficient factory system, an industrialized one, he sees himself as a cog in a machine-like production process.

The potters who have tried working in city factories do not like to do so. They say the work is hard and debilitating, that working so hard can cause rheumatism and fevers. Their complaint is not concerned solely with the physical effort expended on these jobs, for frequently it is less than that in a day's plowing or eight hours on the lettuce fields of Salinas, California. They object to the factory work because they feel driven and pursued. They are not likely to institute a factory system in their own home. The Ceramic Museum in Tlaquepaque has for some time been interested in setting up a pottery workshop in Tonalá and employing some of the more skilled potters. This suggestion has been met in the typical Tonalá way—silence when confronted directly by museum personnel, hostility and gossip when the subject is brought up among themselves, and a complete lack of cooperation. When the workshop idea was pushed, one of the potters stopped dealing with the museum completely, another had a disagreement with one of the employees and from then on refused to open her door to him. Several of the potters said they would not and could not work under such conditions, for as long as they worked in their own homes they were their own bosses; others said they could not work outside the home because they had to be able to interrupt their pottery-making to farm.

This is not to say that the individual Tonaltecan will not be caught up in a factory system, but there are some preconditions before this can happen. The villagers must come to view time as a commodity, to be added to the cost of production. At present few, if any, Tonaltecans see it this way. Human effort is considered important for judging value, but not the lapse or passage of time. They would neither understand nor accept the view of Benjamin Franklin which Weber (1958: p. 48) quotes as containing the spirit of capitalism "in almost classic purity": "Remember that *time* is money. He that can earn ten shillings a day by his labour, and goes abroad, or sits idle, one half of that day, though he spends but sixpence during his diversion or idleness, ought not to reckon *that* the only expense; he has really spent, or rather thrown away, five shillings besides."

The pottery producers would also have to believe that increased production and the money gained thereby are primary goals to which other activities must be subordinated. At this point in their history their economic system does not work in that way. Fulfillment of noneconomic obligations, the reinforcement of social ties, and participation in ceremonial and religious functions all intrude upon the attainment of an economic goal, for the average Tonaltecan is concerned less with getting more goods than with maintaining himself and his family within the matrix of the life of the community.

The relationship between the workers in the factory and their employer is also overlaid with noneconomic considerations; they are not simply contractual, for the obligations of employer to employee and vice versa are manifold. Don Pascual Aldana is a very important man in the community; not only is he the owner of the only pottery factory, but he is also a community leader. During his term in office as presidente municipal, the town hall was modernized. The old arches which bridged the sidewalk were eliminated, for they were assumed to be symbolic of Tonalá's *atrasado* (backward) status, and a façade of typical mid-century provincial architecture was substituted: a row of high small windows, a curvilinear, false-gable roof line, and a town clock to mark the passage of the quarter hours. Don Pascual was also one of the leaders in the initiation of the present water system; indeed, many Tonaltecans now believe that he was single-handedly responsible. He is generally considered to have been one of the best presidents Tonalá has had. Nevertheless, during and after his term he was subjected to the usual criticism given all town officials; since then he has refused to serve again and has seemingly lost his former interest in being active as a town leader.

Although he is no longer an active political leader, he still feels that he owes an obligation to his employees. He often is the godfather of his employees' children at the time of their first communion. Even when he does not officially assume this role, he provides candles and flowers for the ceremony. Since first communion ceremonies are performed once a year when the archbishop visits Tonalá, the Aldana Pottery Factory sends a pickup truck loaded with flowers at that time. The factory also sponsors a soccer team, and uniforms are provided by Don Pascual.

Employees of the factory feel that they can depend on getting a loan from Sr. Aldana when they are in dire financial straits. Since few Tonaltecans are able to save money, any illness can be a devastating financial blow. There are many people in town who make a business of making loans, but interest rates are very high (up to 20 per cent per month). If a villager feels he has established a patron-client relationship with someone, he prefers to borrow money from that person, for the existence of the personalistic social relationship may lower the interest charged or wipe it out entirely. Don Pascual is probably the person most frequently called on for this kind of service;

by the godfather ceremony he becomes a fictive kinsman of all his employees, past and present, and one always feels that one can depend on aid from a compadre. Sometimes these loans are not paid back, but the obligation involved is written off if the borrower can perform some other kind of service for the lender.

It is clear that the relationship between Don Pascual and the workers in the factory is not the universalistic, functionally specific one that would obtain between employer and employee in an industrial society. Tonaltecans prefer to have this kind of relationship to the man, rather than to the status, to be involved as persons rather than role-players in an economic system. They are uncomfortable about social relationships which are businesslike and purely contractual, which are not enriched and complicated by personalism.

The townspeople's relationship with the Ceramic Museum of Tlaquepaque is characterized by them as cold. This state museum was set up in 1954 with the cooperation of the Instituto Indigenista and the Instituto de Antropología e Historia. Its primary goal is the rehabilitation of the local ceramic industry; in order to do this effectively it maintains several display rooms to acquaint visitors with the long traditions of pottery-making in this region. The museum buys part of the production of the Tonalá potters and sells to visitors, to the Museo de Artes Populares in Mexico City, and to gift shops and decorators. It is interested in reestablishing Tonalá as a major center of handicraft through the encouragement of the production of articles of high aesthetic value and through the introduction of new techniques and new designs. It tries to stimulate Tonaltecans to produce fine objects by assuring the potters a steady market for this kind of goods. But the potters reinterpret the actions of the museum people, for they cannot place the role of the museum employee in the social world they know. The museum officials are not paternalistic employers like Sr. Aldana with whom they are bound in a complicated set of patterns of obligations; they are not fellow townspeople to whom one is neighbor and kinsman; they are not even anthropologists who live in the village and who are caught up in the system of exchanges of favors and courtesies. There is nothing in a Tonaltecan's previous experience that makes him understand disinterested benevolence.

The difficulties are many and varied. The trouble begins with the fact that the museum people are city people, trained primarily to view the final product as the ultimate goal, rather than being primarily concerned with the potter. Sometimes they behave with an air of condescension which does not escape the Tonaltecans—who are on the lookout for such an attitude anyway. Little things make a lot of difference. For instance, Pablo Savedra said that when a group of Mexico City photographers came to take the pictures which appear on the walls of the museum and in Isabel Marín de Paalen's book, the director of the museum told Pablo that he was to go out to mine clay so that photographs of this process could be made. He had been given no forewarning and was in the midst of working on an order of pottery; he resented the high-handedness—particularly since he had not been offered money for his services. The museum was unable to get the cooperation of the Tonalá potters for that phase of the picture-taking, and men in Tlaquepaque were hired to pose for the pictures. When this news reached the town (or perhaps it was invented in the town), there was even more resentment: if Tlaquepaqueños were paid for posing, why were Tonaltecans not?

Pablo Savedra's attitude is not completely unrealistic;

the museum personnel often acts as if the Tonaltecans were "their potters," having been granted to them by the National Institute of Anthropology. When the museum was first established, the director tried to push the potters who were producing quality ware to sell only to it. This move has been unsuccessful, for as one potter put it, "It is difficult to produce enough museum pieces to provide tortillas for dinner." So they continue turning out the souvenir ashtrays that the museum feels debase the taste of the potters.

Tonaltecans gossip about the museum people as they gossip about their townspeople: they accuse them of setting up a monopoly, of carrying on illicit romances, of profiteering with the work of the potters, of incompetence, of overcharging; but although they may occasionally seem silent and truculent, in face-to-face contacts they greet the museum employees politely, often graciously.

The difficulties the museum has in dealing with the potters do not stem only from the somewhat patronizing attitude of the personnel, on the one hand, and the misinterpretations of the roles by the potters, on the other. The museum often has to try to guide the work of the potters in order to insure a growing market; they must try to encourage imagination and inventiveness—and this is something much more difficult than putting the phrase down on paper. Since the pottery craft is learned in the home from the family's elder members, traditional modes of behavior tend to be emphasized. There is a premium put on imitation and copying. As a result, most potters tend to think of particular vessels as things that *are,* not as objects which one can adapt to the needs of the moment; thus there are things one can think of as survivals, such as the lines or "waists" around *jarros* (mugs) which have no function, which are not the result of a necessary step in production and which are not decorative, but which are considered to be a necessary adjunct to the jarro.

In addition, pottery-making is not thought of as a vocation to be learned in school or through lessons: it is a *destino* (a fate), and it is particularly the destino of certain families in Tonalá. If an outsider manages to learn to make satisfactory pottery, it is a source for constant comment. Many Tonaltecans feel that the artist attached to the museum cannot possibly know anything about pottery, for he has been around Tonalá for only a few years. Any attempt by the museum personnel to tell Tonaltecans what or how to produce is met with hostility.

The museum's job is not an easy one: the market it is selling to is one operating along the usual commercial lines, but its producers are still using methods of production, forms of work-organization, and goals that do not fit well with rational economic practices. For instance, the museum, faced with time limits to fill orders, may find that delivery is next to impossible because of religious holidays or because the potter has sold all his production to someone who came around ahead of the museum truck. Trying to work as a commercial mediary between Tonalá and the world of business is not easy—a fact well known by the middlemen who count on large markups to cover the cost of loans to potters, failure to meet deadlines, and general frustrations. Trying to work as an artistic mediary between Tonalá and the changing world of fashion in art is almost impossible. It would take a genius at diplomacy to convince the potters to abandon traditional ways of working; and it would take a genius in the triple fields of art, psychology, and anthropology to accomplish the museum's stated aims: to invent designs that (1) fulfill the artist's need to express himself, (2) draw upon the artistic traditions of this region, and (3) appeal to the ever-changing market for objects of art.

Most of the pottery produced in Tonalá is sold to *comisionistas* (commission merchants). These men make agreements with individual potters to buy certain kinds and amounts of pottery, sometimes advancing money. To *habilitar* (to finance) is a common practice; the advance presumably is to cover the cost of materials, but nowadays it is always in the form of money rather than actual raw materials. Prices are set after a period of bargaining, although within certain limits there are traditional prices. The prices are responsive to the market situation, even to the national economic picture; at the time the peso was devalued, the potters raised their prices immediately. If the middleman's final offer is too low for the potter to consider the work profitable, he may try to make a deal with another merchant. Sometimes, however, he is tied to one particular individual because of a previous loan or because of a moral obligation to a compadre. In Talcott Parson's terminology there are several particularistic factors involved in the potter-comisionista relationship, which on the surface looks like a simple contractual tie: personal obligations on the part of the potter because of money advances (which are often personal loans as much as advances for material), traditional seller-buyer relationships because of complementary specialization (e.g., a potter who makes fine decorative ware would sell to a comisionista who sells to urban gift shops), and compadrazgo (cf. chap. viii). The potter prefers this kind of relationship for he feels it suits his needs better. The middleman ordinarily is patient about the date of the delivery of an order, and the potter feels he can take time to farm or that he has some kind of insurance against an emergency.

Many middlemen are local people; some are merchants who also deal in grain or groceries. Others specialize in pottery. But there are also dealers who come in from the outside—agents from gift shops in Tijuana or Nogales who drop by Tonalá on their way to Mexico City to buy items to sell, owners of Guadalajara shops around the Libertad Market who sell thousands of chocolate mugs and jars to city people, and representatives of North American gift shops. The Ceramic Museum, seen from the potters' point of view, acts like a comisionista, even though the stated aims of the institution are broader than those of the merchants.

Sometimes the comisionista market is in a slump, and a potter will find his usual outlets closed. One of the ways out of this dilemma is to take the pottery to Guadalajara and sell it at the Mercado Libertad or to the owners of souvenir shops in that city. The potters prefer the middleman system—some say because they hate to waste a day or so a week marketing pottery in the city, others because they can get paid in advance.

On Thursdays and Sundays pottery is sold in the town square. The women of the pottery-making households carry baskets full of mugs, water bottles, and cooking pots to the plaza. They set out their wares in traditional spaces which are arranged according to cuartel. People from Cuartel 1 occupy the corner across from the town hall, so this is the section one would go to for water jugs in the white-on-red Tonalá tradition. Cuartel 2 displays its ware along the western street of the square; here there are more water jugs and toys, piggy banks and miniature dishes. On the opposite side of the square sit the women from Cuartel 3 with neat rows of large and small mugs; while the sellers from Cuartel 4 arrange their cooking pots on the northeast corner of the plaza. Little if any fine ware comes to this market; an occasional burnished gray and beige piece is sold here, but only if it is cracked or chipped and rejected by the comisionista; famous makers of ollas also sell to wholesalers rather than at the traditional market.

Some outsiders also sell in Tonalá on market days. The potters of El Rosario bring huge sackfuls of water bottles on the bumpy bus-ride from their nearby village, and great quantities of these botellones are sold. Tonaltecans are contemptuous of these water bottles, for they are formed from a vertical mold and have a seam down the middle; in Tonalá it is claimed that El Rosario bottles frequently split; nevertheless they sell well, for they are very pleasing to the eye: a buff-colored background is decorated with stripes and flowers in varying tones of earth-red.

From Tatepozco just down the hill from Tonalá come the makers of cántaros, bringing their large jars by donkey and setting them out on the sidewalk in front of the drugstore. Small merchants who buy up seconds in the pottery factories of Tlaquepaque set up shop wherever they can find room on the inside of the square.

The buyers at the local market are frequently city people who have come to the town to pick up some bargains in cooking ware, a few curiosities, and pork cracklings. Owners of Guadalajara pottery shops and booths, as well as small merchants from other parts of the state, come with pickup trucks and buy up entire lots of chocolate mugs, piggy banks, and casseroles. An occasional United States tourist visits the plaza, wanders around, snaps pictures, and buys a few items.

At present Tonalá potters feel that they can sell all the pottery they can make, and indeed the market is very good. They sell to giftware shops both in the United States and Mexico; they sell to the museum, to a Mexico City department store, to Mexican tourists, to North American tourists, to housewives from the city, and to each other. There are outlets for decorative ware and for utilitarian pieces, for the finest objects they can produce and for seconds. This is not a time in the history of the town when they are haunted by a vanishing market, as has been true in the past. When their market was shrinking, they were forced into changing what they produced. They have been quite adaptable in the last two or three decades to the needs of the market. There were times in which they turned out thousands of flowerpots decorated with sleeping Mexicans with big sombreros, leaning against a nopal cactus; when Esperanza Velásquez was there, they painted bright yellow palm trees on pale yellow *tecomates* (a gourd-like shape seldom made nowadays); Isabel Marín de Paalen (Marín, n.d.: p. 46) refers to a pseudo-Aztec period in this century. Tonaltecans make what they can sell, even if an occasional potter finds his tastes differ from those of his clients. Don Prudencio, for instance, refused to turn out the sleeping-Mexican style flowerpots, for, he said, any idiot should know you can't lean on a cactus, and a house is bigger than a man. When a dealer from Los Angeles brought the Sánchez brothers a large picture of a gorilla to be reproduced in clay, they felt it was too ugly and told the man they were unable to make a copy. These instances are unusual, however; ordinarily the demands of the market prevail.

The greatest impetus toward change is the market. Within the limits mentioned above, a Tonaltecan potter will make any clay object which can be made by the molding method he is accustomed to and by using his kind of kiln. These latter two limitations are more important than the aesthetic one. What changes is the shape of the object or the kind of decoration used; what remains the same is the technique of manufacture, the division of labor, and the organization of work. Since these latter factors are those which control the amount of production, Tonaltecans tend not to produce more, even when the market could absorb more.

On the other hand, a few potters play around with copying objects made elsewhere or inventing new shapes, even though there is no direct economic pressure toward innovation at present. Jorge Saltillo, for instance, tried to make black ware like that made in Oaxaca even though he is able to sell all the traditional ware he makes; his father was considered a great innovator, and he feels a certain pressure to continue the family name for invention. He is still thinking in market terms, however, for he knows that black ware sells well in Tlaquepaque, but he does not know what would sell well in the United States or at the border, for his personal acquaintance with the market is limited. Most Tonaltecans who experiment with what are for them new shapes and objects do so in terms of what they know sells in Tlaquepaque or in the parts of Guadalajara with which they have contact. Consequently, they try their hand at producing porcelain-like knickknacks which are copies of Japanese copies of European figurines, or black or red vases adorned with gold dragons *à la chinoise*.

It is through this latter kind of innovation and experimentation that some potters try to increase their income. The alternative of increasing their production is occasionally pushed for short periods when they have specific short-term needs (e.g., to help buy fireworks for a fiesta, to provide a daughter with a white dress for first communion, to get the necessary money for admission to the bracero lists), but they increase output by working longer hours rather than by reorganizing the work into a more efficient pattern, and the going gets too heavy for the lengthened workday to become a standard practice.

There remains still another way of increasing income: through raising the prices for the goods sold. Unfortunately for the potters, present marketing practices make this alternative almost impossible. Each individual potter strikes a bargain and makes a contract with a middleman; the latter can take advantage of the competition between makers of similar ware, and often the rivalry between the potters is sharp enough that they are not sure at just how low a price the others are selling. To make matters worse for the potter, he is often in debt to the wholesaler. All in all, from the point of view of price-setting, the wholesaler holds all the cards.

If the potters of Tonalá were able to form either a marketing cooperative or some kind of corporation, they could probably command considerably better prices for their wares. This kind of move would put them in effect within the boundaries of the national industrial system; now they are peripheral to it—potters whose income is not high enough for them to participate actively in the national consumer market even though their products are sold both nationally and internationally.

About thirty years ago an attempt was made to form a potters' cooperative. The immediate stimulus came from a group of artists and intellectuals in Guadalajara, including Licenciado Guadalupe Zuno, Dr. Atl, and José Clemente Orozco, all of whom were interested in encouraging folk arts and bettering the standard of living of the craftsmen. The cooperative was organized with a set of officials elected from among the potters in the village. Participants were to deliver their pottery to the cooperative's warehouse, and the officers were to sell the ware of the members. As the story is told now, the venture had a short life. The officers allegedly sold their own products in preference to those of other potters; many villagers say that they lack the education necessary for running such a concern. Most villagers hold the opinion that a cooperative, a company, or a committee can only be successful if decision-making authority rests in the hands of an outsider. Otherwise the officer is committed to decisions that give preference to his relatives or his compadres. This point of view is a rather realistic one, considering the wide distribution of *personalismo* in municipal, state, and national government.

Other matters also helped cause the failure of the cooperative. Tonaltecans have few regular means of cooperation other than along the lines of kinship and reciprocal relationships. The organization of specialization in pottery is such that most families related patrilineally are turning out very similar wares. If one were to utilize the existing kinship bonds as a base for a pottery cooperative, one would have formed a series of agencies each producing a particular kind of ware. But such cooperatives would not be economically feasible, for they would be too narrowly specialized. In addition, in time it is likely that a cooperative of water-jug makers would hold a position vis-à-vis a cooperative of cooking-pot makers comparable to the old barrio system at its height.

Generalized cooperatives would have to be formed across barrio lines, an almost impossible task in a town where one suspects the motives of one's next-door neighbor and, even with more fervor, those of one's affinal relatives or of strangers across town. An outsider can see that what is called for is a pan-Tonaltecan cooperative in which the participants are recruited universalistically (i.e., any potter from town is eligible to join and every potter occupies the same status), and relationships are functionally specific (i.e., within the cooperative one works as a potter and member, not as a relative or compadre). Such an internal structure would be essential for the maintenance of the cooperative for any length of time; otherwise it would break down under the usual charges of inefficiency, ineptness, and dishonesty of the leaders, and the withdrawal of support of the membership. Such a structure would also be necessary if the cooperative is to survive in the outside economic world, for it would have to deal efficiently in an economic system of developed markets, accurate bookkeeping, and elaborate credit system. Even if a traditionally oriented Tonaltecan cooperative could be formed, it seems doomed to fail as a marketing agency.

While I was in the field, a rather halfhearted attempt was made to organize another cooperative. The school director, a native of Tonalá who had worked for many years in the federal school system in the state of Sinaloa, returned to head the school in his home town. He is a man much interested in improving the level of education and the living standards of his fellow townsmen. Shortly after his return, he suggested to some of the potters that it would be to their advantage to organize themselves. He outlined a program which would cover the various facets of buying raw materials, accumulating capital, and selling at an improved price. He felt that the cooperative could be begun quite modestly by having the participants set aside a small percentage of their production each week and investing these pieces in a cooperative; thus no money outlay would be necessary to start the enterprise going. Part of this capital accumulated over a few months' period could then be used to buy glaze and pigments in wholesale lots and to set up some simple machinery for crushing clay. Out of the cash obtained from the sale of the rest of the pottery a small amount should be set aside consistently toward the formation of a fund to provide loans for emergencies, a substitute for the comisionista's financing. The remainder would then be paid back to the potters according to the amount of pottery they had delivered to the cooperative.

Everyone agreed at first at the meeting that this was indeed a magnificent plan, covering several of the needs of the potters. However, as usual, the discussion soon reverted to the old themes: how could an individual member be sure he was not being cheated? what could prevent those in charge from running away with the group's funds? what assurance did they have that the officers would not play favorites? After the adjournment of the meeting, talk and gossip along these lines continued for a week or so. During this period the school director discovered that many people had assumed that he was interested in the plan because he wanted to obtain advantages for his pottery-making relatives. Because of the gossip and because of the burden of his school duties, he refused to take over the leadership of the group. He also hoped that if he let things alone for a while individual potters would take some initiative and help form a democratic potters' organization. Nothing came of the venture. After interest in the gossip had disappeared, no one assumed any leadership, partly for fear of being criticized as the school director had been, and the whole matter was forgotten.

The formation of any kind of business company would face similar difficulties. No single potter accumulates enough capital to set up a factory; he would find it necessary to ally himself with several others in order to have a fund large enough to work with. This kind of alliance would encounter the same kind of problems of distrust and lack of support that a cooperative would have to face. The additional factor that acts as a deterrent to the formation of a pottery company is that most potters, if they are able to accumulate any capital at all, prefer other alternatives. Often such money is spent on religious rituals or on hospitality. A few men, who are interested in reinvesting capital, put it into other kinds of ventures which will mean more prestige. Pottery-making is very low on the ladder of prestige so far as occupations go; if a Tonaltecan wishes to move upward, he invests in land or cattle. Occasionally he may try his hand at being a middleman, but he tries hard to get away from the production end of the ceramic industry. Perhaps Don Pascual was able to maintain prestige because he was an outsider and not a member of any of the low-prestige pottery-making families. The Tonaltecans themselves cannot repeat his success story.

Tonaltecans differ from most of their rural neighbors in that pottery-making represents a major part of the town economy, but they share with the villagers around them the idea that the proper occupation of nonurban people is farming. The village view is that agriculture bolsters the family's economic security and adds to a man's prestige. Everyone agrees that it is far better to grow the corn for the family's tortillas than to buy it with money; and most people also agree that if one has a small patch of land, it is better to grow maize than to raise a crop for the market. To be a farmer on one's own land is to be a permanent, independent citizen of the town; to become a farmer when one has been a potter only is to gain esteem in the eyes of one's neighbors; to till a patch of land—owned or sharecropped—is an occupation worthy of a man.

The cultural focus on agriculture is reflected in the close tie between the agricultural calendar and the ceremonial year. On January 17, the day of San Antonio Abad, domesticated animals are blessed, the men bringing livestock and horses, the women and children pigeons, chickens, turkeys—or even pet dogs—to receive the blessings of the priest. May fifteenth is the day of San Isidro, patron of farmers, and all Tonalá turns out to celebrate. Boys are dressed in *calzón blanco* (a traditional white pajama-like garment) and carry seeds and ears of corn. Girls, decked out in flowing skirts and embroidered blouses, carry baskets of tortillas, fruits, and bottled soft drinks, as if on their way to take dinner to the men in the fields. Women bring seeds to be blessed, representing all the major crops of the region: corn, peanuts, beans, and squash. Men lead their work oxen, which have been elaborately adorned with necklaces of corn, strings of peanuts, and brightly colored paper bows. After the blessing there is a special Mass celebrated before the church altar laden with gourds, corn, and peanuts. Later in the year, if a drought threatens the crop, the farmers organize processions to take the image of San Isidro out to the fields so he can see the barren lands and, taking pity on them, intercede on their behalf. From winter to harvest, the raising of animals and the tending of crops provide the occasions for much of the town's ceremonial life.

Many Tonaltecans are farmers. In 27 per cent of the households (288) farming was listed as a primary or secondary occupation of the head of the house. The figures do not tell the whole story, however, for within that group fall the middle-class owners of fertile lands yielding corn to sell as well as corn to eat, the potters who have a *milpita* (cornfield) in the back corral, and the rancheros of the Third Cuartel who work only in agriculture—whether on their own land, on that of another as a sharecropper or wage laborer, or in the United States as a bracero. The census takers were frequently given the response "cattleman," "agriculturalist," or "farmer" to the question about occupations, but these responses were not always in accord with the common meanings of the terms. A man with two or three milk cows would list himself as a *ganadero* (cattleman); a day laborer with one small plot of land he was sharecropping would prefer to consider himself a *labrador* (farmer). Clearly the respondents were trying to increase their prestige by emphasizing their agricultural activities because farming enhanced a man's status while pottery manufacturing or brickmaking did not. Only 173 households (20 per cent of the total) were supported solely by agriculture. The rest derived part of their income from pottery-making (97), services such as selling or driving buses (16), or manufacturing (2).

Quantitative information on size of holdings and amount of land worked was unfortunately impossible to obtain. The municipality, the state tax office, and the federal ejido agency do not have accurate and up-to-date records on such matters. For an anthropologist to begin inquiring about subjects related to amount of taxes due the government or to illegal use of ejido lands would have made further fieldwork impossible. Consequently, I must rely on impressions rather than established facts on the subject of land tenure.

The fields around Tonalá are held under two kinds of land rights: *pequeña propiedad* (small property) and ejido (communal land). The former represents the largest amount of land in use. The average plot is small, ranging from about two to fifteen hectares, but since some individuals own many such plots which they have obtained through purchase or inheritance, there is considerable difference between the amount of holdings of various *pequeños propietarios.*

Ejido lands in theory belong to groups within the community, not to individuals. The constitution of 1917 provided for the breaking up of large haciendas by bestowing or restoring lands on the petition of a group of farmers, who were to cultivate the property in order to support their families. The lands were to be held communally and apportioned to individuals to work. According to law, the individual has use rights, while the ejido retains the right of reassigning the land on the death of the holder. Unused ejido land is to revert to the federal government, while renting out or sharecropping ejido land is cause for loss of use right. The holders of communal lands form a corporate body, electing a set of officials to conduct ejido business and obtaining credit on an organizational, rather than an individual, basis. Administratively, the ejido system is tied directly to the federal government, bypassing all state agencies.

In the 1920's two ejidos were formed from the hacienda properties lying to the west and the southeast of Tonalá. The land division was carried through peacefully. There was no opposition by the hacendados, there was no destruction of hacienda property, and there were no armed disputes over new allocations as there were in many parts of Mexico when ejidos were formed after the Revolution. The ejidos soon had difficulties, however. Most of the ejidatarios of Tonalá were not primarily farmers and could perform agricultural work at only a very low level of efficiency. In addition, Tonalá drew lands which were poor, eroded, and in some cases suitable only for grazing goats. Finally, there was considerable opposition to the whole revolutionary program. Many Tonaltecans were convinced that the land-parceling was immoral and constituted an attack upon the sacred rights of private property; some of them felt that if they accepted ejido land they were stealing from the rightful owners. Antagonism was especially strong in the western half of town, and the ejido formed there had a brief life. Much of its lands are now rented by other Tonaltecans for crops or the grazing of the cattle of pequeños propietarios, although doing so is illegal.

The ejido of the eastern half of town still exists, but it undertakes few activities as a unit. It was formed in 1927, when several communities—Tonalá, San Martín, El Salto, Tatepozco, and Los Puestos—were given land from the holdings of the Hacienda de Arroyo de Enmedio. Some of these lands had been *tierras de riego* (irrigated lands) which until then had yielded two crops annually—wheat in the dry season, and corn in the rainy season. After fractionization the irrigation system broke down, for it was difficult for a body composed of five ejidos from five different communities to administer it. The irrigated fields became dry-farming plots, and the growing of wheat was abandoned.

Early in the history of the ejido it received a loan from the Banco Ejidal to buy work oxen, plows, and other implements. Some ejidatarios are still using the tools obtained at that time. Those who own no oxen must rent them, for there is no cooperative sharing of animals, tools, labor, or equipment on the basis of ejido membership. Oxen are rented from the ejidatarios or farmers at the prevailing price of ten pesos per day or three to five hectoliters of corn plus the care and feed of the animals if rented by season. Arrangements for borrowing tools or for getting labor services are made according to ties of friendship and compadrazgo rather than on an ejido basis. The ejido has made no effort to obtain money for new tools or machinery nor have its members availed themselves of the agricultural information and advice obtainable from the Department of Agriculture. Under federal ejido laws, if they form themselves into a credit association, the ejido would be eligible for a loan from the Banco

Ejidal, but they have not done so. The ejido has not been prosperous, partly because it fell heir to poor lands or lands not suitable for subsistence maize-growing and partly "through lack of unity," according to both members and observers.

At present there are sixty ejidatarios, each of whom holds four hectares of *tierra de temporal* (nonirrigated land). None owns any sizable plot of pequeña propiedad, although some rent or sharecrop the lands of others. Many are also potters and add to their meager agricultural income by engaging in small commerce, for even in the best years four hectares will not supply a family with maize to sell as well as to eat.

The history of the Tonalá ejido is yet another example of the problem the town faces: low productivity linked not merely to poor technology or insufficient information, but to that lack of organization Banfield characterized as "amoral familism" (Banfield, 1958).

The pattern of ownership or rights over land is enmeshed in a variety of land-use patterns. Land may be farmed by the owner, by his employees paid in money wages, by *medieros* (so called from the custom of dividing the yield in half), sharecroppers who are financed or given credit by the landlord's providing seed and oxen, or by sharecroppers for whom he provides only the land and from whom he receives one-third of the yield.

Although Tonaltecan farmers primarily grow corn, beans, and squash for their own consumption, some also plant peanuts or extra plots of corn for the market. With the exception of the large landowners, they prefer to plant peanuts only if they also have a field planted in maize, for having one's own milpita is seen as a form of insurance. In addition, they profit only slightly from the benefits of favorable years or high prices in the national peanut market, for there is a single agent buying all the peanuts in the municipio on behalf of a vegetable oil company in Guadalajara.

A few of the most prosperous farmers own tractors, but the overwhelming majority use teams of oxen to pull simple metal-tipped plows. The agricultural practices are those common to central Mexico: two plowings at right angles before planting, two *beneficios* or cultivations to heap the soft earth around the cornstalks, the cutting of the leaves and stalk above the developing ears to provide food for the livestock, and finally the *pizca,* the harvesting of the mature corn.

If the farmer has not previously committed part or all of his crop (see chap. x) he brings home the harvested corn. Out of his gross yield he gives the priest the 10 per cent that forms his *diezmo* (tithe). Frequently, however, there are other claims on this crop also. He may owe a third or half to the landlord if he is sharecropping; he may have borrowed money or obtained credit from a storekeeper pledging part or all of his crop to repay the debt. Several comerciantes are corn wholesalers in addition to being storekeepers or owners of mills, and buy the grain for cash or obtain it by advancing loans against future harvests. Corn is not sold on the open plaza. Since a large proportion of Tonaltecans engage in farming, there are few retail buyers of maize at harvest time. Consequently, corn-selling becomes a monopoly of those who have facilities for storing grain and who have sufficient capital to be able to invest and wait for their returns.

Along the highway just outside of town there have sprung up since 1959 a few *granjas* (farms, as contrasted with ranches of fields). Most of the land in question is not arable, for it is located on a knoll where erosion has been extensive and there is neither much topsoil nor natural vegetation. The owners, all of them from Guadalajara, have acquired these properties in the last few years in order to set up chicken farms, the latest style of gentleman farming fashionable in the region, but the problem of obtaining sufficient water has prevented further development. In 1960 two granja owners had built bungalows on their property and were using them as weekend retreats. The *granjeros* have little contact with the Tonaltecans. They bring their supplies out from the city and hire no local people. An instance of one of their few contacts with the community illustrates both the distance and exploitative aspects of the city-town relationship.

One of the granja owners had built a modern house on his land and ordered his first supply of chicks, when it became apparent that all attempts to drill for water had yielded only a series of dry holes. Knowing that the pipes connecting the Tonalá water pump with the town ran near his property, he made a private arrangement with the plumber in charge of the pump and tapped into the main pipe for the town water supply. Water was always scarce, and it soon became apparent to several of the main subscribers to the water system that they were receiving even less than usual. Their complaints grew loud enough so that the Water Committee went to the pumping station to investigate. The cause of the drought was readily apparent. The plumber was ordered to close off the bypass to the granja, but no legal action was taken against either the granjero for illegally tapping the town water system nor the plumber for aiding and abetting the action.

All around Guadalajara granjas are springing up short distances from the suburbs of the city. In many cases they become profitable enterprises, specializing in raising chickens or in growing flowers for the city market. They are often also country homes and vacation houses for urban dwellers. The latter pattern may continue around Tonalá, which enjoys a slightly cooler summer climate than Guadalajara, but the Tonaltecan granjas are unlikely lands for intensive agricultural development.

X. BE BORROWER AND LENDER

THE GOODS which make a colorful display in the plaza on Thursdays and Sundays represent only a part of the volume of the materials changing hands. Distribution is not limited to the market place, although that is its most flamboyant and easily observable form. Even a preschool Tonaltecan child knows that certain kinds of goods are bought on the plaza, others from shops, and others are attainable as gifts, not purchases.

The simplest exchange system is based on what Mintz calls "the horizontal market" (Mintz, 1959: p. 21) or Polanyi refers to as "reciprocal distribution" (Polanyi, Arensberg, and Pearson, 1957: pp. 250ff.). There are no prices involved, for A gives something to B with the expectation of getting goods or a service in return in the future. The lines which the exchange follows parallel other dyadic social relations: that is, distribution of certain goods is based upon kinship relations, compadrazgo (co-godparenthood, see chap. viii), and friendship. The exchange relationships, rather than being the impersonal ones of the market, are part of the matrix of the total social relationships of the town.

These exchanges validate and support the existing social ties. They also provide a mechanism whereby new relationships can be entered into and old ones gradually allowed to wither away. A rural family deciding to settle in town, or the occasional family from Tlaquepaque coming to Tonalá in search of cheaper housing, are acknowledged after a brief residence by being sent a few pieces of fruit, a basket of peanuts, or a plate of festival food by a neighbor. This courteous and hospitable gesture initiates the new Tonaltecans into the networks of social and economic relationships. When a newly married couple sets up an independent household, the existence of the new unit is recognized by the same means. On the other hand, friendships which have cooled and compadrazgo relationships which have become burdensome—even relationships between uncongenial kinsmen—can be de-emphasized by failing to keep the chain of exchanges going or by delaying the return of a gift. The reciprocal exchange system thus serves as a flexible mechanism adjusting the social structure to new situations.

Reciprocal exchanges also perform two more clearly economic functions. In the first place, they may increase the total inventory of goods available to the individual—particularly in the case of certain goods which are almost always exchanged in this manner: fresh fruits, locally grown vegetables, and festival foods. Individuals tend to specialize in giving particular goods. Celerino has a guamúchil tree; when the fruit is ripe, he sends some to the compadre Juan. Juan's wife is famous for her tamales.

The next time she makes some she sends a basketful to Celerino. The exchange may take a form other than that of a voluntary gift. Celerino has a few hens; Juan becomes ill with a persistent cough, and his wife decides he needs an eggnog to strengthen him; she sends to ask Celerino for an egg. Under ordinary circumstances Celerino cannot refuse the request without breaking the existing relationship. It is by this kind of exchange that one regularly obtains things like plums, *tunas* (the fruit of the prickly pear cactus), *zapotes,* chayotes, and those two seedpods that provide "fruit" at the height of the dry season—the *guaje* and guamúchil. Eggs and chickens are sometimes exchanged in this way also. Most of these items are only seldom available in the market in the plaza or in the grocery stores. Exchanges involving the giving and receiving of different kinds of goods increase the degree of interdependence among the residents of the town.

Secondly, reciprocal exchanges can be seen as a form of credit. This fact stands out when individuals exchange the same kind of goods rather than different ones. The distribution of pork when a pig is killed demonstrates the principle. There is no way to preserve meat in Tonalá: no freezing or refrigeration, no knowledge of the *charcuterie* techniques used among European peasants to process fresh meats. Beef and pork can be turned into *cecina* (jerky) by air drying, but most of the flesh from a pig must be consumed immediately. Consequently, the effective way of storing or "banking" meat is to give pieces of it to one's relatives, friends, and neighbors, knowing that they too raise pigs which will eventually be slaughtered. By this system everyone participating can expect to receive fresh pork periodically. Mintz (1959: p. 22) emphasizes the general importance of the credit function of "horizontal exchanges," and certainly Tonalá customs provide another instance of the interrelation between reciprocity and credit.

In addition to reciprocal gift-giving, goods are also exchanged by purchase. There are fundamentally two types of markets—the free market in the plaza where prices fluctuate according to supply and demand, and the set-price market in which competition is limited and prices are affected by elements other than supply and demand. The latter market includes most of the transactions involving money that take place between fellow townspeople. Such exchanges are characterized by particularistic, functionally diffuse ties between buyer and seller, since one is buying from a friend, a compadre, a neighbor. At the moment of the economic transaction the buyer is aware of and concerned with the seller in several roles. The seller likewise sees before him not only a customer, but a man who is his youngest son's baptismal godfather, who borrowed his saw and returned it with a broken handle, who was elected treasurer of the Association of Guadalupe, who has an extravagant and careless wife. The various aspects of the customer are weighed to form the seller's judgment of the social status of the buyer, and it is this status which helps determine price and amount of credit. Price comes to be fixed at what the status will bear.

Functional diffuseness enters in another way also. Trading relations tend to have a binding force. They become patterned in the mold of other social relationships in the town. Buying regularly from a certain vendor becomes a social as well as an economic obligation, for the buyer and seller can be seen as traditional client and patron; they can also be seen as participants in the validating of social relationships through buying and selling. If one regularly buys a liter of milk from Don Manuel, one is expected to continue buying a liter daily. To fail to do so—even for what seems like a valid reason to the buyer—means that he may be denied the milk the next time.

It is the goods of strategic importance in local consumption which are distributed through this kind of exchange; thus, corn, rice, beans, and coffee are sold under conditions which tend to discourage the free fluctuation of prices. Goods that are always in scarce supply, such as milk and, to some degree, wheat bread, are also not sold in the free market. The first clue to the set-price feature is that for these goods there is no haggling; everyone knows what the traditional and "reasonable" limits are, according to season and status. The second clue is that any individual has a limited number of sellers with whom he deals. The market is neither random as to persons nor fluctuating as to prices.

What then determines the price for these goods? In the first place, for items like milk and plain bread there are existing ceiling prices, fixed by the government, but rarely supervised and enforced outside the city. Secondly, this market is tied to the credit system. One buys staples regularly from a small grocer with whom one has established credit, so that when cash is scarce one can still obtain corn for tortillas and matches to light the fire. Once a consumer owes money to a particular storekeeper, his choice from whom to buy is limited. It is easier to continue buying where one has open credit, a fact obvious to extenders of retail credit the world over. It is also possible that if one takes a large share of his cash business elsewhere, his creditor may demand payment on the debt. In addition, if the debtor attempts to buy on credit from a storekeeper with whom he has not dealt regularly in the past, the seller is likely to assume that he has used up all his credit with his traditional dealer and is a bad financial risk. All these factors discourage the formation of functionally specific market relationships.

Thirdly, the set-price market, like the reciprocal exchange system, is imbedded in the network of extra-economic social relations and bolstered by the obligations attendant thereto. One is ordinarily expected, for instance, to buy from merchants in the immediate vicinity; to go further afield without some overriding reason (e.g., to buy from a relative) is considered disloyal to the neighborhood. Large grocery stores cluster around the plaza, but small *tendejones* dealing in rice, matches, salt, soft drinks, and cigarettes are found everywhere. Since these small shopkeepers operate on very small sums of capital and can extend only limited credit, a single small store cannot provide sufficient goods or credit to serve even one town block. Consequently, there are some areas where there are stores on all four corners and one in the middle of the block as well—all offering identical goods (cf. Ward, 1960). Neighborhood loyalty also means that each cuartel is likely to duplicate the services offered in the others. Thus there are tailors, dressmakers, curers, barbers, and bakers in each barrio, drawing clients only from within the cuartel.

The fourth factor helping to maintain relative price stability is that of the merchant's self-interest. Both he and his customers agree that he is in business to make money. No one expects him to sacrifice a profit because of a particularistic tie with a client. Indeed, in the Tonaltecan view of things he would be a fool if he did not look out for his own financial interest. Philanthropy is honored only in church and in theory; in practice it earns little approval. Given the constant scarcity of certain goods with a high demand and given the adherence of the merchant to a goal of making as high a profit as possible, one would expect that the price of items like milk would rise continuously. It does not, however. It varies seasonally, rising slightly higher during periods when pasture is scarce or when the weather is extreme, but staying constant from one year to the next. One cannot explain this fact on the basis of the influence of the city market or of official prices, for Tonalá neither supplies milk to the city, nor is it feasible for townspeople to buy milk there, nor do inspectors check the actual prices charged. The ceiling on milk prices is influenced indirectly by the regional market, but it stems more directly from the nature of the demand —high, constant, but dropping off abruptly at the point where outlay for milk represents too large a share of the family income. In 1960 a liter of milk at one peso fifty centavos represented one-eighth of the daily income of a farm worker. An abrupt and steep rise in price would effectively eliminate the demand; Tonaltecans would do without milk and would go back to relying on atole, coffee, and various infusions of herbs as they did in the past. The milk seller would be out of business.

The three factors mentioned above—particularistic ties, credit, and both formal and informal price ceilings—all work against the formation of a free market in transactions between town dwellers. The system operates on another set of principles, however, which may be characteristic of local peasant markets in general: it depends upon face-to-face relations for its maintenance, it tends toward decentralization or localization of services, it produces the multiplication of small distribution units, it institutionalizes both the items traded and the persons involved in the exchanges. On the whole, it militates against innovation and favors traditional patterns of economic behavior.

The market which brings together as participants people

from different communities meets on Thursdays and Sundays in the plaza. The bulk of the goods sold consists of Tonaltecan pottery and water bottles and jugs from the nearby villages of El Rosario and Tatepozco. Goods for Tonaltecans to buy are also brought to the market from other communities. Farmers from San Gaspar sell vegetables and flowers, vendors from San Martín bring their specialties—mangoes, guamúchiles, brooms, and honey—while Guadalajara dealers in dry goods display lengths of flowered dress material, rebozos, and bandana handkerchiefs. The Tonalá market thus provides a wide range of pottery vessels to the buyer from outside the pottery-making region and a diverse selection of goods from other areas for Tonaltecans.

The buyers and sellers in this market come together specifically for the interchange of goods. Seldom do they know each other in other social contexts. Prices are set by haggling and derive basically from the interrelationship of supply and demand, except for the general understanding that one can adjust the range of bargaining according to the social status of the buyer—haggling always begins with a higher figure if he is a North American or Mexican tourist. Credit is not extended, for it is assumed that the risk is too great if lending occurs outside the web of face-to-face relations, where the fulfillment of financial obligations can be supported by informal social sanctions.

Transactions in the plaza on Thursdays and Sundays fit the classic model of the market: buyers and sellers are random as to persons, they enter into functionally specific relationships, and prices fluctuate in relation to supply and demand. This market brings together members of different communities in a temporary integration for specific, economic purposes, but it does not create other kinds of social ties. The plaza commerce serves the town needs of buying and selling and provides color and movimiento in the lives of its residents, but it does not contribute toward welding the communities of the region together into a single social unit.

While the industrial economy of Guadalajara impinges upon the traditional one of Tonalá in some phases of marketing, the town economy operates within the context of a preindustrial society. There is little accumulation of capital, and available capital is invested in short-term enterprises. Production is organized according to traditional rather than strictly rational considerations. Economic relationships are embedded in the matrix of social relations in general, for economic roles are caught up in the network of reciprocal obligations which hold the townspeople together.

There are some specific implications in each of these patterns of economic behavior. Banfield (1958) has pointed out that the Italian villagers he studied conceived economic projects in terms of short-term goals. The fact that the Tonaltecan economy is characterized by such goals accounts for many facts of daily life. The potter makes contracts from week to week. His wife buys daily the food for that day in a permanent market of small stores and booths in the plaza in quantities so small as to astound and amaze an American housewife: a slice of a head of cabbage, fifty grams of coffee, a teaspoon of sesame seeds, for example. Her husband buys his pottery supplies in small amounts at a time. Consequently, neither his selling nor his spending patterns allow him to budget his income or to handle any large sum of money. In such circumstances, to be economical means to avoid spending; the concept of thrift is tied up with minimum expenditure rather than with maximizing income. One does not have drying sheds built for pottery; one does not spend money on tools when a burlap sack, a piece of tin, and a length of fiber will do the job. This short-range expenditure of income affects the pattern and standard of living in many ways, for it prevents the townsman from setting up facilities for storing quantities of raw materials, fuel, or food; it also blocks the formation of any sizable amount of capital for reinvestment. It makes it difficult for him to economize in the sense of manipulating the resources at his disposal in order to obtain the greatest economic advantage.

It also means that in the expanding national economy Tonalá provides a poor market for consumer goods. The blandishments of advertising reach the town primarily through radio, and awaken mild curiosity rather than new demands. Similarly, sellers in Guadalajara see little reason for setting up business in Tonalá. Hardly any Tonaltecan buys much furniture, a few buy appliances, and the majority provide themselves with only one outfit of clothing at a time. Thus far the potential consumer's market is undeveloped and untapped. The new industrial economy expands despite the Tonalás of the nation.

The credit system is also bound up with short-range activities—a penny precapitalism, one might say. Borrowing sometimes consists of credit buying of a quarter kilo of sugar, two Pepsi Colas, or a box of matches from the local grocer, while repayment is done piecemeal as the debtor has an extra peso or two at his disposal. Other forms may involve weekly commitments, essentially because that is the way the pottery industry is structured—as credit with the pottery middleman or loans from compadres and friends expecting repayment after market day. For the same reason, vendors who sell shoes and cloth to Tonaltecans on time send collection agents once or twice a week (in some cases even daily), thus accommodating the urban institution to the realities of town economics.

The important exception to the short-range, small-credit pattern is the borrowing and investment connected with agriculture. Such credit must of necessity be tied to the agricultural season. Consequently, loans secured by a forthcoming crop are usually extended in May, when the farmer needs funds for seeds, and are repaid in October or November after the harvest. Loans based on crops may, however, fall into the short-term category. The month or so before the harvest comes in is a time when money is particularly short for many Tonaltecans. The preceding year's corn is almost gone, and frequent rains interfere with the air-drying of pottery. Individuals may be forced to borrow money, mortgaging their forthcoming crop, or they may sell a large proportion of the unharvested corn at prices considerably lower than what they could get later. Even if they manage to hold off until after harvest, most farmers are sufficiently hard pressed for cash so that they must sell immediately. The market is glutted with corn, and the price is very low. Few farmers store the year's crop until they can get a more favorable price, for they lack both funds to tide them over until later and storage facilities in which to keep the grain. Thus far government subsidies and warehousing for corn have not affected the small farmers of Tonalá.

As has been pointed out in some detail above, economic relationships both in production and marketing overlap with noneconomic roles. This fact helps maintain a kind of market for goods that differs from that of the national economic system in that prices and credit do not fluctuate in response to market conditions alone. An unexpected and often overlooked result, however, is that the nonmarket reciprocal exchanges make available for the individual consumer a wider range of some goods than he would otherwise have. My impression is that the Tonaltecan diet, limited though it is, is more varied than that of the unskilled urban worker in Guadalajara.

The interlocking of economic and social obligations also affects the labor market. Hoselitz (1960: p. 229) points out that the "preservation of the extended family in the economic realm acts as a strong preservative of particularistic attachments in the distribution of economic roles and hence prevents the rapid development of an open, generally accessible labor market." He says (p. 227), "The maintenance of a system characterized by strong particularistic cleavages in its social structure is associated with the persistence of certain supporting structures. Chief among them is the role of the family and kinship in general, and its function in the allocation of economic roles and social status."

Although Hoselitz cautions that his generalization may only be valid for India, it seems to me to apply to Tonalá as well. The fact that production units in both agriculture and pottery manufacturing are family units tends to work against the formation of a free labor market. It does not prevent it, of course, for there is some wage labor in both kinds of enterprises. Both the social rifts existing in the town which set one Tonaltecan in opposition to another and the web of social obligations which integrate the town as a whole (chap. viii above) emphasize "particularistic attachments" and help keep the old system going.

At present neither the patterns of action nor the world view of the Tonaltecans are those "to which commitment is required if economic development is to be pursued" (Moore and Feldman, 1961: p. 13). The situation is not static, however. The increase of sweatshop factories in town will increase the number of wage laborers and enlarge what can only euphemistically be called a "free labor market." The influence of industrial patterns of work and allocations of time will grow as more Tonaltecans seek work in the city, but there is no indication that they will affect either pottery or agricultural enterprises. Nor is there any reason to expect the shrinking of either of these kinds of production, for the one is advantageous so far as regards security of income and the other so far as concerns prestige within the present value system. The willingness to store goods and amass capital and the acceptance of the idea of investment in relation to long-range returns are prerequisites for any internal development. These factors would not necessarily develop as an automatic response to the conditions of city work. Indeed, city wage-workers are part of national industrial economies although in many countries they neither store, nor invest, nor often plan ahead. One can expect that these aspects of the Tonaltecan value system will remain the same long after wage labor dominates the Tonalá economy, and that economic development will remain the monopoly of middle-class urban entrepreneurs.

XI. THE CHANGING TOWN

THE MOST STATIC of villages change. Many things are different from the way they were twenty years ago: most houses are lighted by electric globes, some are served by a municipal water system, and the town is connected with the city by buses that run every fifteen minutes. The mere listing of these facts, however, paints a misleading picture. Tonalá is not the village that chose progress; it is a town to which a few things have happened.

About 1940 the previous curate and some of the more substantial citizens from around the plaza organized a company for the distribution of electric power. They bought the power from the Chapala Electric Company of Guadalajara, and themselves became the first subscribers. This is the only instance in Tonaltecan history of the carrying through of a long-term corporation. Part of its success rested upon the speed with which Tonaltecans accepted the idea of having electricity in their homes. Electricity meant radios, and radios provided a source of entertainment for the potters who worked at home. Guadalajara salesmen came to Tonalá with radios to demonstrate. They offered package deals including the cost of having the wiring installed, and all on easy payments. Today the sound of music and soap operas issuing from every house is evidence of the efficiency of the selling. Other things that come with electricity are less important, however. A single naked globe inside the entrance of the house provides enough light to find one's way around, and occasionally a home-coming bracero brings his wife a gift of an electric iron. No one uses electric power in any phase of pottery production except in the factory where clay is crushed in a ball machine.

The same people who are on the list of the original subscribers of electric power appear on various other lists of innovators. The first bicycle, the first automobile, the first mill for grinding nixtamal for tortillas, the first radio, the only washing machine, the first kerosene stove, the first gas stove, four out of the five existing bathrooms, four out of the six television sets—all belonged to people found on the list of innovators who first subscribed to the Tonalá electric company. Two characteristics of these innovators appear time after time: either the people are outsiders who have moved into the town, or they belong to the local middle class. They are comerciantes (usually storekeepers) or landowners; they are not potters. This particular group of people can be classified as generally "progressive" within the limits of town culture: in some cases the women work or help run the family business, and their houses are "modernized" with tile floors in the opening reception area and windows with glass panes facing the street. Theirs is the middle-class standard of living and mode of spending. It is also directly tied to practices within the city. Insofar as they are financially able, they emulate the ways of the provincial middle class to which they feel they belong.

Other Tonaltecans do not acquire the outward symbols of middle-class status. First, they often lack the money necessary to buy an automobile or a gas stove. But, in addition, even when they can afford some of these items, they do not. There are strong pressures toward living like the average villager, for to do otherwise, to imitate the ways of the people of the plaza or of the city is to be presumido, a sign of disloyalty to the town and its standards. There is also the danger of awakening *envidia* (envy), for an envious neighbor can harm one through slander or witchcraft. In most of Tonalá the innovator, the upwardly mobile, the social climber, is a laughable rather than a respected figure.

The difference in attitude of the "middle class" and the potters is pointed up by an examination of the list of water subscribers. The Vasconcelos family, for instance, one of the most "progressive" families in Tonalá, paid privately to have a pipe run a full block from the end of the main to their houses when water first came to the village in 1945. The inhabitants of the 100 block of Javier Mina, however, who needed only to connect their faucets to the main at the corner, preferred filling water jars at a public faucet in the neighborhood. In March of 1960 the Water Committee had the public faucet removed in the hope of forcing all the townspeople to have house installations made. For a while the people along Javier Mina said they really had no need of a water system because of the water in the wells of their patios (during the rainy season the middle of this block is a marsh), but by April the wells were dry. There was some talk of having water put in, but each family hesitated because they did not wish to make the first application and have to pay for the pipe to the corner. When we left the village at the beginning of August, no one on the block was a water subscriber. That this reluctance is not due simply to a lack of money can be shown by the fact that some of the families have been paying between two and three pesos for water daily from water sellers, spending eighty to ninety pesos monthly. The water bought in two months would have paid for the installation. The people of Javier Mina prefer to continue buying from water vendors rather than to pay for pipe which would benefit their neighbors. Neither did they make any effort to get together and divide the expense. The situation continued despite the fact that four houses are occupied by patrilineally related Fernándezes and two by Salcedos; the Martinez and Sotano households on the same block are related to the Fernándezes by affinal ties; these kinship ties are reinforced by bonds of compadrazgo. But in Tonalá, kinship—real or fictive—is seldom a sufficient source of the solidarity required for group action.

Nevertheless, even "conservative" Tonaltecans gradually accept new items. Braceros may not bring home an urgent desire to install a bathroom in the family home, but they do come back with new hat styles and a liking for denim trousers. Vendors of hot cakes, spelled *quéquis,* offer their wares in the plaza on Sundays alongside the sellers of tacos and tostadas. Many of the symbols of the international industrial world can be seen in the village: Pepsi Cola, juke boxes, and movies enjoy a great popularity. Trucks rather than donkeys carry away Tonaltecan pottery. Comic books bring Donald Duck, Red Ryder, and Mandrake the Magician into the village. Old people say that life in the village has changed most in that one can travel to the city easily, for their grandsons can now work in the city, and they can buy items which are unavailable in the village. Old women stress the fact that few housewives grind their own corn or make their own tortillas. The advent of nixtamal mills and tortilla shops has greatly lightened their household tasks and also has provided wage employment for women. Older people complain, as everywhere, that the younger generation has too much freedom, while the young people feel that the town restricts its youth. However, the two sets of standards are not so far apart that any youthful rebellion can be expected. The differences involve comparatively minor matters such as what is the respectable distance for partners to maintain in dancing the polka and two-step, or whether straight skirts and short sleeves are really indecent. The young people still share most of the village values and adhere to the village patterns rather than city ones.

All these changes, however, are essentially matters of stylistic shifts rather than changes revolutionizing the traditional social system of Tonalá. Neither the Pepsi Cola nor the comic books increased the acceptance of new concepts of social roles. At the present stage in its relationship to the modern industrial world, Tonalá checks innovations which would threaten the existing society. The fear of arousing envy in one's neighbors, of being made to look foolish, of being gulled, dampens initiative and inhibits experimentation with new modes of acting.

Occasionally an individual, more ambitious and daring than his fellow townsmen, will try to attain a social position different from that of his father. Such a decision involves at least two breaks from the customary Tonaltecan way of life: (1) he must act as if mobility were possible, as if the world of individual achievement stressed in school and in the official ideology of the Revolution were meaningful to him, and (2) he must act within the expectations of the national, rather than merely the town, culture. The old way of moving upward was through the priesthood. In the past, this was probably the primary route of social mobility, but nowadays few Tonaltecans choose the priesthood as a life career. In 1960 there was only one student from Tonalá in a seminary, a fact rather disturbing to the local curate. The present careers chosen by Tonaltecans eager to leave the "destiny" of pottery-making involve secular rather than religious training. Several young men have been trained in the city for mechanical jobs. Individuals in two families have received scholarships to study music and are pursuing careers as instrumentalists in the Guadalajara symphony orchestra, one as a concert pianist. The most frequent vocations chosen, however, are as teachers and accountants. Education at normal or commercial schools is required for these jobs, and several Tonaltecans have gone as far away as the state of Nayarit for their training.

Except for the mechanics, who can commute to their jobs, the other new occupations involve leaving Tonalá first for training, subsequently for work, and eventually for residence as well. The new careers followed by the sons of the town do not function for communicating the urban culture to Tonalá. When the pianist or teacher returns home, he slips back into his old position so far as the townspeople are concerned, and they expect him to conform to town customs. To do otherwise is to become alienated from one's old companions. In neither case do the Tonaltecans at home take on city ways or city values as a result of the visits of the prodigal sons.

Occasionally an ambitious Tonaltecan decides to enter the new economic world by becoming an entrepreneur, although this is an economic role usually reserved for the middle-class town members: the storekeepers (however humble), the owners of land, the middlemen in grain or pottery. The entrepreneur's success is often restricted by his limited business experience and by the persistence of the pattern of short-term investments at minimum risks. José González, for instance, returned from a stay in the United States as a farm laborer with a small sum which he intended to use to set himself up in a business with more prestige than pottery-making. First, he tried lending money, but one of his customers complained to the priest that he was being charged 6 per cent *per month.* The priest summoned José, pointed out that the interest rate was exorbitant, and that usury was an un-Christian practice. José meekly acquiesced, but on leaving the priest, stormed over to the debtor and demanded immediate payment. He felt that the priest's real objections were connected with his being a potter attempting to engage in an enterprise usually handled by comerciantes, and after the irate debtor had paid him off with money borrowed elsewhere, he withdrew from the loan business.

Next, he considered buying cattle and becoming a ganadero. He bid on a small herd that was for sale, but the animals were sold to an old friend of the owner. José again felt that he had purposely been excluded because the people of higher social rank did not wish him to be one of them. His feelings probably reflected his own worries about being presumido and awakening envy.

His last sally into the business world lay closer to his own area of competence. He decided to sell pottery at a festival in western Jalisco. Since he owned no means of transport, he was restricted to taking what pottery he could manage to squeeze as baggage on a bus, but the quantity he could carry was not sufficient to yield a profit. José had not estimated his expenses nor his gross income in advance, so on his return he was faced with the disillusioning fact that he had lost rather than made money. He decided the role of entrepreneur was not for him and returned to the United States as a farm laborer.

The Tonaltecan entrepreneur tries to improve his social and economic position by moving into traditional status positions: he buys a small plot of farm land, sets up a minuscule store in which he sells soft drinks and matches, and acquires a cow or two. He does not enter into enterprises which are concerned with production nor does he move into an intensive exploitation of the low-prestige activities he customarily engages in. The average Tonaltecan does not expect to get rich or powerful by becoming a pottery tycoon.

In the twenty years since the end of World War II there has been continual growth of the industrial system of Guadalajara. Nevertheless, in those twenty years there have been no revolutionary changes in Tonalá. Its traditional mode of life has gone on, its citizens expect tomorrow and next year to be much like today, and most people, although at times beguiled by a view of "progress" or of attaining an urban standard of living, are reasonably content with things as they are. The view that traditional society has attractions of its own in the slow pace of change, in the regularity of expectations, in the self-consistency of its operation and the smooth functioning of its institutions, can entrance the observer and the participant so that he fails to see the small evidences of new developments. Most of the townspeople do not see that inevitably the industrial developments of Guadalajara will affect Tonalá.

While Tonalá continues in its old patterns, the city has already established outposts. The granjas on the edge of town bring their owners out on weekends to play gentleman farmer, but, while they take land out of the hands of Tonaltecans, they do not provide work, a market for town goods, or taxes to the community. The sweatshops form another kind of outpost, but in each case Tonalá is viewed as a locale, a territory in which to place an enterprise; in each case, the intention is to exploit the locale rather than invest in it. The economic units are set up to interact with the life of the inhabitants in a minimal way, for the absentee entrepreneur, like the absentee landlord, feels little responsibility toward the community in which he operates his business. The general disdain with which Tonaltecans are regarded by city people intensifies this attitude, while it deters other entrepreneurs from investing in town enterprises. Urban investors do not see Tonalá as a possible market, for the town has already been categorized as "backward" and "Indian." Tonaltecans are seen as a cheap source of labor, not as potential buyers. The "sweatshop stage" of city-town relations is not likely to last long, however, for Tonalá will soon be involved in another kind of relationship with Guadalajara.

The southeastern boundaries of the city creep closer and closer to Tonalá as it expands. The two municipalities are contiguous, but as yet three miles of field and hamlet separate the town from the proletarian sectors of the city. As the urban lower-class population increases, the city approaches the boundary of its municipality and moves closer to Tonalá. Since the nearest area of Guadalajara is what one might euphemistically label the "low-rent district," the town is likely to find itself surrounded by that hodge-podge of squatters' shacks, *vecindades* (tenements), and undeveloped real estate developments typical of the peripheries of other industrial cities of Mexico. In the last ten years the former town of San Andrés was swallowed up in this fashion; a settlement of weavers became a community of factory workers, waiters, and porters. The city population is still growing. Soon the pottery village of El Rosario and the truck-farming community of San Gaspar, both just over Tzihualpilli's hill from Tonalá, will have been engulfed by the expansion of Guadalajara. Now in 1965 the new highway which is to encircle the city, the *anillo periférico* (peripheral ring), passes through all of these communities. At the crossroads of the highway to Querétaro and the road to Tonalá, speculators have set up a card table at which they sell city lots made out of what were cornfields only four years ago. Of the possible ways in which industrialization will affect Tonalá, this is the one most likely to revolutionize the town. Because of its particular geographical position in relation to the city, Tonalá does not provide us with a model of how a town responds to the process of industrialization as a separate unit through all the stages of development from a peasant community through an industrial town. It does, however, provide us with another instance of the process of urbanization we have seen in the Western World throughout the nineteenth and twentieth centuries. In time Tonalá will be another Charing Cross, another Harlem.

GLOSSARY

Abnegada, self-sacrificing.

Atole blanco, a traditional drink made of ground corn and diluted with water or fruit juice to a gruel-like consistency.

Barrio, neighborhood or quarter of the town.

Barro colorado, red clay.

Barro de olor, aromatic clay.

Botellón, water bottle.

Bracero, a farm laborer who comes to the United States to work under contracts supervised by both the Mexican and United States governments.

Calzón blanco, the traditional garments of the farmer, white muslin pajama-like trousers.

Cántaro, a large water jar.

Cargador, literally "bearer," but in Tonalá refers specifically to a religious official undertaking certain financial and social obligations in the Festival of the Holy Cross.

Castillo, a pyrotechnic set piece, consisting of a light framework to which fireworks are attached.

Comadre, co-godmother, the godmother of one's child or the mother of one's godchild.

Comal, clay or sheet metal griddle.

Comerciante, businessman or shopkeeper; in Tonalá the term includes both owners of substantial businesses and the gatherers who sell firewood and cow dung for fuel.

Comisión, a religious official undertaking part of the financial and social obligations in the Festival of the Holy Cross.

Comisionista, middleman; in Tonalá the term refers specifically to pottery middlemen.

Compadrazgo, the system of fictive kinship operating through co-godparenthood.

Compadre, co-godfather, the godfather of one's child or the father of one's godchild.

Consuegro, co-father-in-law, the father of one's child's spouse.

Corredor, an inner part of the house which is open on one or more sides but is sheltered by a roof.

Cuartel, a quarter or ward of the town.

Ejidatarios, members of ejidos.

Ejido, communal land (see chap. ix).

En la calle, in the street.

Escándalo, scandal or noisy uproar.

Ganadero, cattleman.

Greta, pottery glaze, lead oxide.

Guamúchil, from Nahuatl *cuauh-mochitl,* Bot. *Pithecolobium dulce* or *Inga pungens,* a characteristic tree in the landscape of Tonalá which bears edible seedpods in the height of the dry season.

Habilitar, to finance; in pottery-making, to advance money to cover cost of the materials.

Hacendado, owner of an hacienda.

Indios feos, ugly Indians.

Labrador, a small, independent farmer.

Macho, the virile, aggressive, male.

Madrina, godmother.

Mesón, inn.

Milpa, cornfield, growing corn.

Milpita, little cornfield.

Mole, a sauce for fowl made from ground chiles, pumpkin seeds, chocolate, and various herbs.

Movimiento, literally "movement," but also connotes noise, people, and color.

Mujer abnegada, the self-sacrificing, dutiful woman.

Oficial, in Tonalá refers specifically to a religious official who undertakes particular financial and social obligations in the Festival of the Holy Cross.

Orilla, edge of town.

Padres de Familia, the parents' association of the local elementary school.

Padrino, godfather.

Pasillo, the passageway in the front part of the house.

Pedida, petition, the asking of the hand in marriage.

Pequeña propiedad, farmland held as small, individual private property.

Pequeños propietarios, owners of pequeña propiedad land.

Pipián, a sauce for fowl made from ground peanuts, squash seeds, and chiles.

Pozole, a soup of pork (including part of the pig's head) and hominy, garnished with chopped raw onions, cabbage, and radishes.

Presentación, presentation, the appearance of a couple before the priest to announce their intention of marrying.

Presidencia municipal, town hall.

Presidente municipal, the elected head of a municipality.

Presumido, presumptuous.

Robo, robbery, bride-stealing (see chap v).

Serenata, band concert and promenade held in the plaza on Sunday evenings.

Sopa de arroz, "dry soup" of rice, tomatoes, broth, and herbs.

Suegros, parents-in-law.

Tarea, task or chore; in pottery-making, the traditional amount made in a day's work.

Tendejones, small corner grocery stores.

Tierra de temporal, farmland watered by seasonal rains.

Villa, town.

Voluntad, will.

BIBLIOGRAPHY

Anesagasti y Llamas, Jaime de

1899 Brevísimas notas de la historia antigua y moderna de Tonalá. Guadalajara, Tipografia Católica de A. Zavala y Cia.

Arensberg, Conrad, and Solon T. Kimball

1940 Family and community in Ireland. Cambridge, Mass., Harvard University Press.

Banfield, Edward

1958 The moral basis of a backward society. Glencoe, Ill., Free Press.

Basalenque, Diego

1886 Historia de la provincia de San Nicolás de Tolentino de Michoacán, del orden de N.P.S. Augustin. México, Edición de la "Voz de México."

Berreman, G. D.

1962 Behind many masks: ethnography and impression management in a Himalayan village. Society for Applied Anthropology, Monograph No. 4.

Bushnell, John

1958 La Virgen de Guadalupe as surrogate mother in San Juan Atzingo. American Anthropologist, 60:261–265.

Diaz-Guerrero, Rogelio

1955 Neurosis and the Mexican family structure. American Journal of Sociology, 112:411–417.

Foster, George M.

1948a Empire's children: the people of Tzintzuntzán. Smithsonian Institution, Institute of Social Anthropology, Publication No. 6. Mexico, D.F.

1948b Some implications of modern Mexican mold-made pottery. Southwestern Journal of Anthropology, 4:356–370.
1953a Cofradía and compadrazgo. Southwestern Journal of Anthropology, 9:1–28.
1953b What is folk culture? American Anthropologist, 55: 159–173.
1961 The dyadic contract: a model for the social structure of a Mexican peasant village. American Anthropologist, 63:1173–1192.

Gillin, John P.
1960 Some signposts for policy. *In* Richard N. Adams, Oscar Lewis, John P. Gillin, Richard W. Patch, Allan R. Holmberg, Charles Wagley, Social change in Latin America today: its implications for United States policy. New York, Vintage Books.

Hobsbawm, Eric J.
1959 Primitive rebels: studies in archaic forms of social movement in the 19th and 20th centuries. Manchester, Manchester University Press.

Hoselitz, Bert F.
1960 The market matrix. *In* Wilbert E. Moore and Arnold S. Feldman, eds. Labor commitment and social change in developing areas, pp. 217–237. New York, Social Science Research Council.

Ingham, John
1965 The Psychology of Machismo. MS.

Lewis, Oscar
1959 Five families: Mexican case studies in the culture of poverty. New York, Basic Books.
1960 Tepotzlan: village in Mexico. New York, Holt, Rinehart and Winston.

Marín de Paalen, Isabel
n.d. Alfarería: Tonalá. Jalisco en el Arte, ed. J.R. Alvarez, Guadalajara.

Mintz, Sidney
1959 Internal market systems as mechanisms of social

articulation. *In* Verne F. Ray, ed. Intermediate societies, social mobility, and communication; proceedings of the 1959 annual spring meeting of the American Ethnological Society, pp. 20–30.

Mintz, Sidney, and Eric Wolf
1950 An analysis of ritual co-parenthood. Southwestern Journal of Anthropology, 6:341–368.

Moore, Wilbert E., and Arnold S. Feldman (editors)
1960 Labor commitment and social change in developing areas. New York, Social Science Research Council.

Mota Padilla, Matias de la
1870 Historia de la conquista de la provincia de Nueva Galicia. Mexico, Imprenta del Gobierno, en Palacio. Publicada por la Sociedad Mexicana de Geografía y Estadistica.

Mumford, Lewis
1934 Technics and civilization. New York, Harcourt, Brace.

Navarrete, Ignacio
1872 Compendio de la historia de Jalisco. Guadalajara, Isaac Banda.

Oglesby, Catharine
1939 Modern primitive arts of Mexico, Guatemala, and the Southwest. New York, Whittlesey House.

Parsons, Elsie Worthington (Clews)
1936 Mitla, town of the souls, and other Zapoteco-speaking pueblos of Oaxaca, Mexico. Chicago, Ill., University of Chicago Press.

Parsons, Talcott, and Robert F. Bales
1955 Family socialization and interaction process. Glencoe, Ill., Free Press.

Paz, Octavio
1961 The labyrinth of solitude: life and thought in Mexico. New York and London, Grove Press.

Pitt-Rivers, Julian
1954 The people of the Sierra. London, Wiedenfeld and Nicolson.

Polanyi, Karl, C. Arensberg, and H. Pearson (editors)
1957 Trade and market in the early empires. Glencoe, Ill., Free Press.

Ramirez Flores, J.
1960 Matrimonio: indígenas de Zacoalco Jalisco en el arte, ed. J. R. Alvarez. Guadalajara.

Razo Zaragoza y Cortés, J. L. (editor)
1963 Crónicas de la conquista del reino de Nueva Galicia en territorio de la Nueva España. Instituto Jalisciense de Antropología e Historia, Serie de Historia, 4.

Romano V., Octavio Ignacio
1960 Donship in a Mexican-American community in Texas. American Anthropologist, 62:966–976.

Siegel, Bernard J.
1962 Biennial review of anthropology, 1961. Stanford, Calif., Stanford University Press.

Simpson, L. B.
1966 Many Mexicos, 4th edition. Berkeley and Los Angeles, University of California Press.

Stanislawski, Dan
1950 The anatomy of eleven towns in Michoacán. Austin, University of Texas Press.

Tello, Fray Antonio
1945 Crónica miscelánea de la santa provincia de Xalisco. Libro IV. Guadalajara, Editorial Font.
1891 Libro segundo de la crónica miscelánea en que se trata de la conquista espiritual y temporal de la santa provincia de Xalisco en el nuevo reino de la Galicia y nueva Viscaya. Guadalajara, Imprenta de "La Republica Literaria" de Ciro L. de Guevara y Cia.

Ward, Barbara
1960 Cash or credit crops? An examination of some implications of peasant commercial production with special reference to the multiplicity of trades and middlemen. Economic Development and Culture Change, 8:148–163.

Weber, Max

1947 The theory of social and economic organization. Translated by A. M. Henderson and Talcott Parsons. Glencoe, Ill., Free Press and Falcon's Wing Press.

1958 The Protestant ethic and the spirit of capitalism. Translated by Talcott Parsons. New York, Scribner.

INDEX